MW00479337

screaming in the castle

screaming in the castle

selected shorter pieces

by

CHARLES NICHOLL

A Common Reader Edition

The Akadine Press

Screaming in the Castle

This COMMON READER EDITION published 2000
by The Akadine Press, Inc.

Copyright © 2000 by Charles Nicholl.

All rights reserved. No part of this publication may be repro-
duced or transmitted in any form or by any means electronic
or mechanical, including photocopying, recording, or any
other information retrieval system, without permission in writing from The Akadine Press, Inc., 141 Tompkins Avenue,
Pleasantville, New York 10570.
Telephone 1-800-832-7323.
On the Internet: www.commonreader.com

A COMMON READER EDITION and fountain colophon are
trademarks of The Akadine Press, Inc.

ISBN 1-888173-99-8

10   9   8   7   6   5   4   3   2   1

contents

foreword

O**F THE** fifteen pieces collected together in this volume, thirteen first appeared in British magazines and newspapers, one was a contribution to an anthology, and one ('Crows') is published here for the first time. They appear unchanged apart from some minor topping and tailing—hard to resist in a situation like this—and some new titles in place of those bestowed on them by that *eminence grise* of all journalism, the sub-editor.

Some of these pieces have a historical or literary bent, and may perhaps aspire to being called essays rather than articles. Others are on more contemporary themes. In the first case one tends to be dealing with texts and documents, in the second case with living people and actual locations, but in the end the winkling out of facts and insights is much the same process whatever the source.

The articles that were contemporary when I wrote them are, of course, no longer so. They are snapshots. The cities of Alexandria and Dublin have moved on, metaphorically speaking. The Glastonbury Festival is no longer quite the gesture of defiance it was in the Thatcher years. My comments on the elections in Panama in 1990 ('Incident at Yaviza') were almost instantly outdated by the US invasion of the country, and the consequent removal of General Noriega, but the bulk of the story is a personal experience which I think is still worth telling. The historical pieces also age: no account of Christopher Marlowe's boyhood is now complete without mentioning Andrew Butcher's recent discovery of him as a nine-year-old—'oneley a boye'—serving in a Canterbury victualling-house in 1573 (see *Christopher Marlowe and English Renaissance Culture,* ed. Grantley and Roberts, 1996). These small caveats aside, I leave the pieces to speak, and readers to judge, for themselves.

I am grateful to Tom Meagher and Chris Carruth of the Akadine Press, and though none of these pieces goes back that far, I wish also to remember those whose encouragement meant so much to me at the beginning, on what was still literally Fleet Street—John Anstey and David Holloway of the *Telegraph,* Tom Hopkinson, and James Cameron.

Charles Nicholl
Lucca,
March 2000

screaming in the castle

screaming in the castle

B **EATRICE CENCI** was—to
take a sample of sound-bites
over the centuries—a 'goddess of beauty', a 'fallen angel', a
'most pure damsel'. She was also a convicted murderer. This
is a charismatic combination, not least here in Italy, and her
name has lived on, especially in Rome, where she was born
and where she was executed in 1599.

The story as it comes down to us has the compactness of
legend. It tells of a beautiful teenage girl who kills her brutal
father to protect her virtue from his incestuous advances; who
resists interrogation and torture with unswerving courage; and
who goes to her execution unrepentant, and borne along on a
wave of popular sympathy. There have been many literary

London Review of Books, 1998

treatments of the story, the most famous of which is Shelley's verse-drama, *The Cenci*, written in 1819. Other writers drawn to the subject include Stendhal, Dickens, Artaud and Alberto Moravia. The appeal of the story is partly lurid—a pungent mix of Renaissance sex and violence; a sense of dark deeds behind the closed doors of a prominent Roman family. It affords a glimpse, in Shelley's words, of 'the most dark and secret caverns of the human heart'. There is also the ethical conundrum it poses, its puzzle of legal guilt versus moral innocence. At the end of Moravia's play, *Beatrice Cenci* (1958), she tells her prosecutors: 'Accuse me if you wish, but I am innocent . . . According to your justice you will certainly be able to prove that I am guilty of my father's death. But you will never be able to prove that I am not at the same time innocent according to another justice—a justice which you cannot know, still less administer.'

The beautiful murderess, the innocent sinner: La Cenci has cast her spell on the imagination—especially on a certain kind of male imagination—and it is with some difficulty that one digs back through the silt of literary sentiment to the event itself, which took place four hundred years ago, in the precipitous little village of La Petrella del Salto, in the foothills of the Abruzzi mountains a hundred kilometres northeast of Rome.

SOMETIME AFTER seven o'clock on the morning of 9 September 1598, a woman called Plautilla Calvetti was combing flax in her house at La Petrella. She heard a confused clamour outside—'shouted words that I could not understand'. She hurried out into the street. Someone she knew called to her: 'Plautilla, Plautilla, they are screaming in the castle!'

The castle stood up on a steep crag above the village. It was known as La Rocca, and certainly today its stubby ruins, overgrown with broom and elder, look more like an outcrop of rock than the remains of a building. It was then the kind of rough-hewn, strategically placed fortress-cum-country-house that a very wealthy and very dodgy Roman nobleman might choose to hole up in when things got a bit hot for him—both climatically and figuratively—down in Rome. This was broadly the case with the current tenants of the building: Count Francesco Cenci, a 52-year-old Roman around whom accusations of corruption and violence clustered like summer flies; his second wife, Lucrezia; and his youngest daughter, Beatrice. The two women were essentially prisoners in the castle, slaves to the Count's brutality, paranoia, and—if the rumours were to be believed—sexual abuse.

Plautilla knew the castle, and its secrets, rather better than most in the village. Her husband Olimpio was the *castellano,* or manager of the castle, and she too worked there as a housekeeper. This was why the villagers were here at her house, shouting that something was wrong—even wronger than usual—up at La Rocca. Olimpio was absent, however.

Plautilla ran straightaway up the steep track to the castle, 'with one slipper on and one slipper off'. She saw Beatrice Cenci looking down at her from one of the windows. She called up to her: 'Signora, what is the matter?' Beatrice did not answer. She was clearly distraught but 'strangely silent', unlike her stepmother Lucrezia, who could be heard screaming inside the castle.

Some men came hurrying down the track. As they passed Plautilla they told her: 'Signor Francesco e morto.' The infamous Count Cenci was dead.

His body was lying in what was called the 'warren', a dense patch of scrub below the castle rock which was used as a refuse tip. It appeared he had fallen from the wooden balcony that ran around the upper storey of the castle. There was a drop of six *canne* (about thirteen metres) into the warren. Part of the balcony had collapsed: one could see splintered wood, though the gap looked small for the bulky Count to have fallen through.

Ladders were fetched. Three or four of the men climbed down the 'wilderness wall' and into the warren. They confirmed that Cenci was dead—despite his fall having been broken by the branches of an elder tree. Indeed, the body was already cold to the touch, suggesting death had occurred some hours before. It was hauled up with great difficulty, roped to one of the ladders, and on this improvised stretcher it was carried to the castle pool, down below the outer gate. A crowd of villagers had gathered, among them three priests. They stared at the mortal remains of the great Count Cenci. His face and head were matted with blood; his costly *casacca* or gown of camel's hair was torn and befouled with the rubbish of the warren: a 'miserable rag'.

It was during the washing of the body, at the castle pool,

that questions started to be raised. As they rinsed the blood off the Count's raddled face, they found three wounds on the side of his head. Two were on the right temple, the larger one 'a finger long'. The deepest and ugliest wound was near the right eye. One of the women deputed to wash the body, whose name was Dorotea, made irreverent comments about the dead man. She thrust her forefinger into the wound with grisly relish. One of the priests, Don Scosso, later said: 'I could not look at it any longer.' Porzia Catalano, another onlooker, said: 'I turned my eyes aside so I didn't have to look, because it frightened me.'

It was not the ghoulish jesting of Dorotea that struck the priests, however, so much as the nature of the wounds. How far their statements were shaped by later knowledge we do not know, but the priests who witnessed the washing of the body all claimed to have recognised instantly that the wounds on Cenci's head had been made not by a fall from the balcony but by a violent blow with a sharp instrument. They thought they had been 'made with a cutting tool like a hatchet' or with a 'pointed iron', or possibly with a stiletto. One of the priests, Don Tomassini, also noted a deep bruise on the Count's arm, above the left wrist.

Thus, even before the dead man's eyes had been closed (or rather, as Don Scosso pedantically noted, 'the left eye, for the right eye was completely destroyed by the wound'); even before the body, clad in a fresh shirt and laid on sheets and cushions from the castle linen-chest, had been carried down the twisting lane to the village church of Santa Maria which was to be its resting-place, it was already suspected that Count Cenci's death was not an accident but a case of murder.

Standing on the site of the castle pool four centuries later, assisted by the conventions of the Hammer horror-movie which this story often resembles, one envisages that moment of dawning recognition, when the assembled villagers fall silent, and their eyes slowly turn back up to the forbidding silhouette of La Rocca, to the 'strangely silent' figure of Beatrice at the window.

THIS BRIEF account, based on statements by witnesses, catches at least something of the reality of the Cenci murder. It is a local event, as all historical events are to begin with; a sudden noisy intrusion into the routines of a late summer morning in La Petrella. This is the event before the dust has settled. Thereafter it becomes progressively distorted by various kinds of partisanship—the police investigation, the extraction of confessions, the hectorings of the trial, the blanket cruelties of the verdict—and then by the obscuring draperies of legend.

The investigation by the Neapolitan authorities (who controlled the province of Abruzzo Ulteriore) was thorough, and even the defenders of Beatrice do not dispute its basic findings. Count Cenci had indeed been murdered, horribly. While he slept, drugged by a sleeping draught prepared by Lucrezia, two men had entered his bedroom. Despite the drug it seems he awoke. One of the men held him down—the bruise on the wrist which Don Tomassini spotted—while the other placed an iron spike against his head and drove it in with a hammer. The two slighter wounds on the Count's head were probably botched blows before the coup de grâce smashed home. They then dressed the body, humped it to the edge of the balcony and threw it down into the warren. Leaving a half-hearted hole in the balcony floor to make it look like an accident, and a mass of 'scene of crime' evidence—blood-soaked sheets and the rest—to show that it wasn't, they rode off into the night.

The two men were Olimpio Calvetti—the trusted *castellano* of La Rocca, the husband of Plautilla and, it later transpired, the lover of Beatrice—and a hired accomplice, Marzio Catalano, a.k.a. Marzio da Fiorani. These were the murderers of Count Cenci, but they were really only hit-men. The true architects of the murder were the Count's immediate family: Lucrezia and Beatrice, his long-suffering wife and daughter; and his eldest surviving son, Giacomo. The latter was actually in Rome when it happened, but his extensive confessions provided the bulk of the case against them. Beatrice was said to have been the most implacable of the conspirators, the one who urged the assassins on when they baulked at the last moment. She refused to confess, however, even under torture.

The judicial process lasted exactly a year, during which time both of the murderers died. Olimpio Calvetti, on the run in the Abruzzi hills—we shift from Hammer Horror to Spaghetti Western here—had his head sliced off with a hatchet by a bounty-hunter. Marzio Catalano died under torture in the interrogation rooms of the Tordinona Prison in Rome. On 10 September 1599, Giacomo, Beatrice and Lucrezia Cenci were executed outside the Castel Sant'Angelo on the banks of the Tiber. Giacomo's death was protracted—he was drawn through the streets on a cart, his flesh mutilated with heated pincers, his head smashed with a sledge-hammer, his body quartered—but the two women walked to their death 'unbound and in mourning garments' and were 'cleanly' beheaded. A not entirely trustworthy account of the execution adds that Lucrezia had difficulty settling at the block because of the largeness of her breasts. A fourth Cenci, Bernardo, too young to be actively involved, was forced to watch the killing of his kin and was despatched to the galleys thereafter.

The affair was a cause célèbre. It echoed briefly through the newsletters of the day: 'The death of the young girl, who was of very beautiful presence and of most beautiful life, has moved all Rome to compassion'; 'She was 17 and very beautiful'; 'She was very valorous' at her death, unlike her stepmother, who was a 'rag'.

THE BALD facts of the case do not go very far in explaining the passionate interest it has aroused. This has little to do with the actual murder of Count Cenci: on that, posterity's verdict is a simple 'good riddance'. It is rather the particular quality—real or imagined—of the person who has become the protagonist, the star, of the story: Beatrice Cenci.

Though there was undoubtedly a continuous knowledge of the case from the late 16th century onwards, the legend of Beatrice Cenci is essentially a Romantic construct. Its origin can be found in a long and highly coloured account by the historian Lodovico Antonio Muratori, in his 12-volume chronicle, *Annali d'Italia*, published in the 1740s. This popular book brought the case to a new generation of Italian readers, and when Shelley arrived in Rome in 1819 he found that the story of the Cenci was 'a subject not to be mentioned in Italian society without awakening a deep and breathless interest.' For Beatrice herself, he added, 'the company never failed to incline to a romantic pity', and a 'passionate exculpation' for the crime she had committed.

Shelley almost certainly knew Muratori's version, and he may also have known an early dramatisation by the obscure and prolific Florentine playwright Vincenzo Pieracci (1760–1824), but the only source he mentions in the Introduction to his play is a mysterious 'old manuscript', which he describes as 'copied from the archives of the Cenci palace in Rome' and 'communicated' to him by a friend. Mary Shelley also mentions this manuscript in her later notes on the play, though exactly what it was, and how much Shelley's historical errors or reworkings were taken from it, is unclear. His version of the murder itself, for instance, is strangely sanitised: the Count is strangled by Olimpio, 'that there might be no blood'. This accords rather better with his idealisation of Beatrice than the messy reality of the murder.

Shelley's poetic heroine, agonising between the impossible alternatives of incest and parricide in tones that sometimes recall Isabella in *Measure for Measure*, is the exemplar of the Romantic Beatrice, and ushers in a parade of doomed heroines in prose works by Stendhal (*Les Cenci*, 1839), Niccolini (*Beatrice Cenci*, 1844), Guerrazzi (*Beatrice Cenci*, 1853)—the latter a work of almost unbearable treacliness—together with shorter essays or treatments by the elder Dumas and Swinburne. In the 20th century the legend has persisted—a film (*Beatrice Cenci*, 1909) directed by the Italian Expressionist director Mario Caserini; a 'Theatre of Cruelty' version, *Les Cenci*, by Antonin Artaud, first performed in Paris in 1934 with Artaud in the role of the wicked Count; and Alberto Moravia's wordy, Anouilhesque play, *Beatrice Cenci* (1958).

Then there is an oral tradition. A typical synoptic version of the story runs: 'her father dishonoured her, and in revenge she killed him by stabbing a silver pin into his ear' (Carlo Merkel, *Due Leggende intorno a Beatrice Cenci*, 1893). Another, recorded in La Petrella in the 1920s by Corrado Ricci, describes her torture: 'they hung her up by her yellow hair, which reached to her knees.' This finds its way into Artaud's play: 'From the ceiling of the stage a wheel is revolving on its invisible axis. Beatrice, attached to the wheel by her hair, is urged on by a guard who grips her wrists behind her back.'

These literary or anecdotal aspects of the legend are closely connected with a visual aspect: the supposed portrait of Beatrice by Guido Reni, which shows a beautitul young girl with brown hair and wide, lustrous eyes. According to tradition, scrupulously nurtured by all the 19th-century writers on the subject, the portrait was taken from the life during Beatrice's imprisonment in late 1598 or 1599. An alternative tradition, taking into account the unlikeliness of the unknown Guido being able to visit her in the Corte Sevella prison, says it was based on a glimpse the artist had of her in the street as she went to her death. Shelley saw the painting in 1818, in the Palazzo Colonna in Rome, and described the face as 'one of the loveliest specimens of the workmanship of Nature':

> There is a fixed and pale composure upon the features; she seems sad and stricken down in spirit, yet the despair thus expressed is lightened by the patience of gentleness . . . The lips have that permanent meaning of imagination and sensibility which her suffering has not repressed . . . Her eyes, which we are told were remarkable for their vivacity, are swollen with weeping and lustreless, but beautifully tender and serene. In the whole mien there is a simplicity and dignity which, united with her exquisite loveliness and deep sorrow, are inexpressibly pathetic.

The portrait was, in Mary Shelley's view, the spark which ignited the poet's interest—Beatrice's 'beauty cast the reflection of its own grace over her appalling story; Shelley's imagination became strangely excited'.

A few years later, the expatriate French novelist and flâneur Henri Beyle, better known as Stendhal, was similarly moved, seeing in the portrait 'a poor girl of 16 who has only just surrendered to despair. The face is sweet and beautiful, the expression very gentle, the eyes extremely large; they have the astonished air of a person who has just been surprised at the very moment of shedding scalding tears.' Dickens found it 'a picture almost impossible to be forgotten', full of 'transcendent sweetness' and 'beautiful sorrow'. In her face 'there is a something shining out, that haunts me. I see it now, as I see this paper, or my pen' (*Pictures from Italy*, 1846). Nathaniel Hawthorne, meanwhile, found the picture 'the very saddest ever painted or conceived: it involves an unfathomable depth of sorrow.' It is 'infinitely heartbreaking to meet her glance . . . She is a fallen angel—fallen and yet sinless' (*Transformations*, 1858).

Despite these plangent and heavyweight endorsements, it is almost certain that the face in the portrait has nothing at all to do with Beatrice Cenci. Guido Reni, a Bolognese by birth, is not known to have painted in Rome before 1608, nine years after her death. In its visual imagery—particularly the turban-like drapery—the portrait is more likely to be a representation of one of the Sibyls, or female prophets. (There is a turbanned Cumaean Sibyl by Guido Reni at the Uffizi.) The girl's extreme youth suggests she is the Samian Sybil, sometimes referred to in classical sources as a *puella*.

The earliest connection of the portrait with Beatrice appears to be in a catalogue of paintings owned by the Colonna family, compiled in 1783—'Item 847. Picture of a head. Portrait believed to be of the Cenci girl. Artist unknown.' In documentary terms this identification, itself tentative, belongs to the late 18th century, to the time of the upsurge of interest in La Cenci arising from the account in Muratori's *Annali*. It is not too cynical to suggest that her name was appended to the picture to lend it a spurious glamour. This seems to have been the result, for when Shelley showed a copy of the painting to his

Roman servant, he 'instantly recognised it as the portrait of La Cenci'.

The painting now hangs in the gloomy corridors of the Palazzo Barberini; it was purchased in 1934 by the Galleria Nazionale d'Arte Antica. The label below it has a question mark after both the artist and the subject, and adds an apologetic note that the painting is of 'poor quality' and is only famous because of its supposed connection with Beatrice. A couple of rooms away hangs the gallery's masterwork: Caravaggio's breathtaking *Judith Cutting off the Head of Holofernes*. In the expression of Judith, resolute but disgusted by the sheer messiness of the operation; in the fountains of blood spurting over the bed-sheets; in the scarcely veiled eroticism—her hardened nipple is painted with great specificity beneath the white gown—one might see an entirely different reading of Beatrice Cenci: not sweet and mournful like the young Sybil, but steeled to a necessary, or perhaps merely expedient, act of butchery. There is no provable connection between Caravaggio's Judith and Beatrice, but it is by no means impossible. Caravaggio was working in Rome at the time of her trial and execution, and the painting is broadly dateable to this period. Perhaps it contains a vein of comment on the Cenci case; it is rather more likely to do so than the dubious Reni portrait, which caused so many flutters beneath the frock-coats of the literati.

In the later 19th century, the case became the object of more serious historical investigation. In some instances the findings contradicted the received pseudo-facts of the legend, though they did little to diminish its popularity. Even sober scholars found it hard to resist the peculiar allure of La Cenci. When a Victorian antiquarian, Edward Cheney, discovered an autograph letter of Beatrice's in a Roman archive, he duly published the text in a learned periodical (*Philobiblon*, Vol 6, 1861). Halfway through his transcription he signals an omission, with a note that states: 'Here the manuscript is illegible from tears having blotted it'. I have seen a photograph of the original document. There is some deterioration of the paper, but no sign whatever that this was caused by La Cenci's teardrops. The bibliophile has suffered that characteristic rush of blood to the head which Beatrice excites in all the historians, particularly male ones.

THE MOST challenging documentary discoveries were made by a tenacious archival ferret, Dr Antonio Bertoletti. In 1879 he published his findings in a slim, refreshingly dry volume, *Francesco Cenci e la sua Famiglia*.

His first discovery was a manuscript volume in the Vittorio Emmanuele library in Rome, headed 'Memorie dei Cenci'. In it he found, in the surprisingly well-formed hand of Count Cenci, a precise register of the births and deaths of his many children. Among these Bertoletti was surprised by the following entry: 'Beatrice Cenci mia figlia. Naque alla 6 di febbraio 1577 di giorno di mercoledi alla ore 23, et e nata nella nostra casa.' So we learn that the beautiful teenage girl of legend, invariably described as 16 or 17, was actually 22 years and seven months old when she died. Her birthplace—'our house'—was the rambling Palazzo Cenci, on the edge of Rome's Jewish ghetto. It is still standing, though split into apartments and offices: one may imagine her passing under its dark archways, lingering by the small fountain in the courtyard, walking up the marble stairs. From the top floors she could see the broad sweep of the Tiber, and on the far bank the drum-like shape of the Castel Sant'Angelo, where she would meet her death. The topography suggests the narrowly circumscribed ambit of her life.

Bertoletti also made a remarkable discovery in his examination of Beatrice's will, or rather—crucially—wills. (The fact that she was allowed to write a will at all puts a question mark over the received view that Pope Clement VIII hounded the Cenci to death in order to swell his coffers with confiscated revenues.) In her first and fullest will, notarised on 27 August 1599, Beatrice left a great deal of money—about 20,000 scudi in all—to charitable and religious causes. She made particular provision, in the form of trusts, for the dowries 'of poor girls in marriage'. She also made a number of smaller bequests, typically 100 scudi, to individual relatives and retainers. What caught Bertoletti's eye, however, was the following clause, and the rather more secretive trust-fund it alluded to:

> Item. I bequeath to Madonna Catarina de Santis, widow, 300 scudi in money, to be placed at interest, and the interest to be given in alms according to the instructions I have given her. If the said Madonna Catarina should die, this legacy is to be transferred to others, on condition that they use it for the same purpose, according to my intention, as long as the person to whom these alms are to be given remains alive.

Beatrice's friend Catarina de Santis is obscurely traceable: a respectable widow with three unmarried daughters (also remembered in Beatrice's will). But who is the unnamed person who is to be the beneficiary of the legacy, according to the 'instructions' given to Catarina verbally but not revealed in the will? The probable answer was discovered by Bertoletti in a hitherto unknown codicil to the will, added by Beatrice on 7 September 1599, witnessed by her brother Giacomo and lodged with a different notary. In this codicil, written two days before her execution, she increases the sum allotted to Catarina to 1000 scudi and specifies the purpose of the bequest as being 'the support of a certain poor boy [*povero fanciullo*], according to the instructions I have verbally given her'. She also adds that if the boy attains the age of 20, he should be granted 'free possession' of the capital. It cannot be proved, but it seems very likely that this 'poor boy' for whom she made such generous and secret provision was her son. If so, there is not much doubt that the father of the boy was Olimpio Calvetti, whose intimacy with Beatrice is noted by many witnesses. The hushing up of a pregnancy may have been one of the reasons for the 'imprisonment' of Beatrice at La Rocca.

From these documents a different Beatrice emerges. The angelic Beatrice of legend, the sweet and mournful girl of the Guido Reni portrait, the spotless damsel (or sublimated Lolita) of the 19th-century romancers, proves to have been a tough young woman in her twenties, probably the mother of an illegitimate child, probably the lover of her father's murderer. This does not, of course, lessen the awfulness of her situation or the tyranny of her father. Nor does it lessen the evils of the sexual abuse she suffered, even if her vaunted chastity is no longer part of that equation. But how much of this is fact? Did her father really violate her, or attempt to do so?

Throughout her interrogation Beatrice maintained that she was entirely innocent of the murder. Her defence was simply that she had no motive for killing her father. It was only later, during the long and crucial summing-up by her lawyer, Prospero Farinacci, that the question of incest arose, as a compelling mitigation of her crime. Corrado Ricci notes sternly: 'in all the trial records from November 1598 until August of the following year—in more than fifty examinations—there is not the slightest hint of any such deed.' There is plenty of evidence of her father's violent temper—it is certain that on one occasion he attacked her with a whip—but no mention of incest.

Then, in her last examination, on 19 August 1599, Beatrice reports her stepmother Lucrezia urging her with these words to kill her father: 'he will abuse you and rob you of your honour.' This seems to suggest that sexual violence was threatened, though the phrasing does not prove that any sexual violence had yet taken place. Ten days later, a former servant at La Petrella, Calidonia Lorenzini, appeared before the prosecutor. (She did so voluntarily, at the request of certain friends of Beatrice's.) In her deposition she stated that a few days before Christmas 1597, she was in bed at 'the third hour of the night', when Lucrezia came in, having been sent out of the bedroom by the Count. A few minutes later, she relates, 'I heard a voice, which seemed to me that of Beatrice, saying: "I do not want to be burned!" I heard nothing else afterwards. The following morning I asked Signora Beatrice what had ailed her when she uttered those words . . . She told me that her father had come into her bed, and she had told him she did not wish him to sleep there.' In terms of statements by witnesses this is as near as we get to first-hand evidence of the bruited incest. The prosecutor was not impressed: he was particularly sceptical that the chattery Calidonia could have kept all this secret from her fellow-maid, Girolama, who knew nothing of it.

Girolama herself gives a vivid glimpse of the brutishness of domestic life in the Cenci household. It was the Count's custom, she said, to have his skin 'scratched and scraped' with a damp cloth—he suffered from a form of mange. This duty often fell to Beatrice. She told Girolama 'that sometimes she scratched her father's testicles; and she said also that she used to dream that I, too, was scratching them, and I said to her: "That will I never do!" ' Girolama also reported that 'Signor Francesco used to go about the house in just a shirt and doublet and a pair of drawers, and when he urinated it was necessary to hold the urinal for him under his shirt, and sometimes [Beatrice] was obliged to hold it; and it was also necessary sometimes to hold the close-stool.' These observations tell us something about life inside La Rocca, but they do not constitute proof that Cenci had raped his daughter.

It may be that the certainty of Beatrice's violation at the hands of her father is the hardest part of the legend for us to surrender, but the truth of the Cenci case, as with many cases of sexual abuse in the family today, will never be known. There are too many untrustworthy sources: suborned and frightened witnesses (witnesses were routinely tortured—hoisted on ropes or stretched on a kind of rack known as *la veglia*—to make them agree with others); documents that may not after all mean what we think they mean; a profusion of folklore and fantasy and poetic wish-fulfilment that has worked its way too deep into the story to be separated out. Francesco Cenci was an arrogant, greedy, lecherous and violent man. There are many reasons why he might have had his head smashed in on a dark night in the badlands of the Abruzzi. Lust for his daughter, credible but unproven, may have been one of them. At least five people were involved in the killing. Each had motives of some sort, but only one (the hit man Marzio, who was in it for the money) had a motive that can be defined with any certainty.

The ethereal legend of Beatrice is at least a kind of memory-device, a retaining of her story in the collective memory. It does not itself contain the complexities and untidiness of the truth, but it serves to remind us of the intense repressions and vulnerabilities suffered by a well-born young woman in late-Renaissance Italy. In this sense, as a representative, as an individual woman who speaks for countless others, Beatrice is a heroine. But to the other questions we want to ask—What was she really like? What really happened and why?—she gives no answer. There was 'screaming in the castle'; there were 'shouted words'. They were audible for a moment above the white noise of history but are no longer decipherable.

mystery at moonlight cottage

THE PHOTOGRAPH has that eerie innocence: a casual event that is about to become a mystery. It shows three middle-aged people on a picnic, one Chinese and two Americans. It is Easter 1967, in the lush surroundings of the Cameron Highlands, a former British hill-station in central Malaysia.

Two of the people in the photograph, Dr T. G. Ling and his American wife, Helen, are now dead. The third, Jim Thompson, was declared legally dead in 1974, but no one can say for sure that he is. It becomes more probable—he would now be 86 years old—but how, when, or why he died is the

Telegraph Magazine, 1992

mystery. This photograph is the last to be taken of him; he disappeared without a trace about three hours later.

Thompson was already something of a legend in Southeast Asia. In the popular press he was known as the Thai Silk King. He settled in Bangkok after the Second World War and began his silk business hawking scarves in the lobby of the Oriental Hotel. At that time, Thai silk was virtually unknown, a local cottage craft. Within a few years—particularly after his designs were used in the musical *The King and I*, set in old Siam— Thompson had turned it into an international industry. When the rich and famous came to Bangkok, they bought silk at his shop on Suriwong Road, and they dined at his superb canalside house, built out of five original houses transported from the old Siamese capital of Ayutthaya. 'There was usually a Thai prince or two there, or an ambassador, or some no-account count,' recalls Barrie Cross, a former manager of the Oriental. 'There were only three menus at Jim's dinner parties. You could tell how important the guests were by what the cook served.'

Jim Thompson, one is often told, was a gentleman. He is sometimes called a snob, though others speak of his hospitality to the young and the broke who drifted into Bangkok: 'If you were interesting, Jim liked you.' Film-footage shows an old-style American expat, tanned and a bit overweight, with a packet of Pall Mall in the pocket of his silk shirt, and a rapid, raspy, corner-of-the-mouth way of talking. He made a considerable fortune, most of it put back into the business or into his almost obsessive art-collecting. He was, and remains, popular with the Thais, a man who fell in love with the country, and who genuinely benefited it. Nath Chaijaroen, for many years his translator, says: 'He was a good man, very diligent. He worked hard and always helped the weavers. They were poor people; now their children go to university, to medical college.' Thompson had a tinge of 'Quiet American' idealism: he once described his work as 'like a missionary, but with better visual results'.

These parts of the Thompson legend remain. His silk company (now owned by a consortium headed by his nephew, Henry Thompson III) is doing better business than ever. An original block of shares, bought in 1950 for $2,500, was recently sold to a Japanese company for $25 million. Thompson silks, some featuring his own designs, command top prices in London, Paris and New York. His 'house by the *klong'* is visited by thousands of tourists every year. But there is also that other, chillier part of the legend, the question that hangs in the rooms of his house: what *did* happen to Jim Thompson that day in the Cameron Highlands?

IN BANGKOK no one has an answer to that question, but everyone has a theory. Many believe that the simplest explanation is the most plausible: that he went for a hike in the jungle, fell into difficulties, and died there. This is the view taken by his biographer, William Warren, and by some of his surviving friends. It is not quite the official story—there is no official story—but it is generally accounted the *sensible* story.

It is by no means the only one you will hear. Some say Thompson was kidnapped. As there was no ransom demand, it was either a kidnap that went wrong, or an abduction for a more complex reason. Others say it was a planned disappearance by a man tired of his own success. Alleged later sightings of him—in Tahiti, Macao, Hong Kong—are mentioned to support this. There is speculation that he was on a mission for the CIA, that he was involved in a planned coup, that he was being blackmailed because he was homosexual, and that he was the victim of machinations within the Bangkok silk industry.

Whichever theory you are listening to, you are sure to be dealt the wild card of the case, which is that a few months after his disappearance, Thompson's sister Kathleen was murdered by an unknown intruder at her house in Pennsylvania.

Some of the theories sound alluring enough over a bottle of cold Singha beer. There is no hard evidence to back them up, yet the same is true of the supposedly simple theory that he got lost in the Malaysian jungle. The search was extensive. At its height, there were 300 people combing the area: the Malay Police Field Force, aboriginal trackers, a detachment of Ghurkas, hotel guests armed with sticks and whistles. The US Army sent helicopters and radar-tracking equipment. In nearly two weeks they found nothing—no shred of clothing, no spot of blood, no sign of a struggle, and no body. The one constant in the puzzle, it seems, is a total absence of clues. As William Warren tells me, 'We really know nothing more about the case than we knew an hour after it happened.'

★   ★   ★

THE CLIMB to the Cameron Highlands is dramatic. At the crossroads town of Tapah, you leave the heat and monotony of Highway One, which runs on down the peninsular to Kuala Lumpur, and switchback up through a lush, steep, misted landscape.

On Friday 24 March 1967, Jim Thompson drove up this road in a taxi, intending—as it appeared—to spend a quiet Easter weekend with the Lings, who owned a cottage here. With him was an old friend, Connie Mangskau, an attractive Anglo-Thai widow in her mid-50s. They had flown down from Bangkok the previous day, spent the night at the Ambassador Hotel in Penang and then hired a taxi for the seven-hour journey to the Highlands. At Tapah they changed cars. There was a brief altercation with two Chinese who wanted to travel with them. Kidnap theorists have found this significant, but it probably was not. Shared taxis were, and are, the norm here. They arrived early in the evening. Ling, a Chinese-born, Harvard-educated chemist who worked for a pharmaceutical company in Singapore, was already there. Helen Ling arrived later that evening.

The Cameron Highlands, first mapped a hundred years ago by the Scottish surveyor William Cameron, became popular during the Thirties as a cool-climate resort for British personnel working in Singapore and Kuala Lumpur. There are three villages, big tea estates, an 18-hole golf-course, and Ye Olde Smokehouse, a country hotel more English than any I have seen in England. Dotted through the greenery are bungalows and holiday houses in hill-station style: vaguely Tudor, with tall gables and timbers. One of these is Moonlight Cottage, set in a twinkling garden of hollyhocks and scarlet salvia. This was the Lings' house. It is the last house up a winding track, 20 minutes' walk from the main road. There has been infilling since Thompson was here, but the cottage is still solitary. According to local lore, the house is haunted. During the Emergency of the Fifties, the place was used by the Communist guerrillas; it is said there were executions on the lawn. Malay shamans attributed Thompson's disappearance to 'bad spirits', as good a theory as some you will hear.

Today the house is owned by Wong Hoke Lim, a Chinese businessman from Kuala Lumpur. When I visited, the drive bristled with warnings—'No Loitering', 'Please Respect Our Privacy'—and pictures of Alsatian watch-dogs, but the place was deserted except for an elderly Chinese housekeeper and a sleepy chow who scarcely managed a bark. The housekeeper spoke no English. The name Jim Thompson, however I enunciated it, meant nothing to her. She watched as I strolled round the garden. She wondered what I was looking for, and so did I. Through the metal-framed windows, past mildew-spotted curtains, everything looked closed up.

On that Easter morning in 1967 Thompson and his friends attended a service at the Anglican church in nearby Tanah Ratah, then drove to the foothills of Brinchang Mountain for a picnic. This was the scene of that last photograph, taken by Connie Mangskau. But here comes the first possible tremor in the story. The picnic was not quite the easy-going affair it looks in the photo. According to Ling, Thompson had suddenly gone off the idea. In an interview with *Asia* magazine in 1974, Ling said, 'After everything had been prepared and we were about to go, Jim changed his mind. He said he didn't want to go, and he urged us to stay home. Well, the rest of us wanted to go, so he finally came along.' Thompson drank no beer with his lunch, and began packing up the hamper almost as soon as they had finished eating. 'He appeared nervous, which was very unusual for him, and he seemed anxious to get back early,' said Ling. 'Who knows why?'

They were back at Moonlight Cottage by about 2.30 pm. Mangskau announced her intention to have a nap. The others, including Thompson, agreed. She retired to her bedroom, the Lings went to theirs, and the last they saw of Jim Thompson he was standing in the living room, preparing—they assumed— to do the same. He did not, however, go to his room. His bed had not even been lain on.

A little after three o'clock the Lings, resting but not sleeping in their room at the front of the house, heard the scrape of an aluminium deck-chair on the verandah. A few moments later they heard footsteps going down the gravel path outside their window towards the drive. (This path is now grassed over, but you can clearly see the line of it.) These were, Helen Ling later insisted, the footsteps of a white man, not an Asian. She was sure she could tell the difference.

This is not quite the last record of him. At about four o'clock, a man matching his description was seen by the cook at the nearby Lutheran Mission bungalow. He came up the track to the bungalow, looked around a bit, and went away again. Shown a photo of Thompson, the cook said she was sure it was him, though she said he was wearing grey trousers, when in fact they were dark blue. Her statement is also problematic because of another witness, at the Overseas Mission Fellowship house, who said that she too saw Thompson at about four. He stood on a small plateau opposite the house for about half an hour, she said, and then he 'just vanished'.

Given the Oriental vagueness about time it is possible that both these sightings are genuine. It takes ten to fifteen minutes to walk from Moonlight to the Lutheran bungalow (which is a dead end), and a little more from there to the OMF house.

WHAT HAPPENED to Thompson after that is the enduring mystery. No one has an answer to that question in the Cameron Highlands any more than they do in Bangkok, but just about everyone I spoke to seemed certain about what did *not* happen to him. He did not die in the jungle. Oh yes, you are told, people get lost in the jungle up here. But—dead or alive—they are always found again.

The terrain here is not, as you might think from reading the reports, the kind of luxuriant, hostile jungle in which disappearance is always possible. It is oak-laurel rainforest. In parts it is like an English woodland in high summer. It was denser then than it is now, says David Fitzstevens, an American aid worker who took part in the search for Thompson, 'but it wasn't that difficult to find your way. Those out there looking for him wondered how he could have got lost'.

Nor was Thompson a novice. He had stayed here before, and knew the area quite well. He had jungle training from his military days. He had hiked through all Thailand on curio-collecting expeditions. Helen Ling remembered him talking on the subject: 'You know,' he said to her, 'if you keep your wits about you, you can never get lost here. All you have to do is find a stream and follow it out, and while you do, drinking its water will keep you alive.'

One theory is that Thompson was attacked and eaten by a tiger. There certainly were tigers in the vicinity, as Helen Robertson recalls. She is the Chinese-born widow of a Scottish rose-grower. She knew the Lings (her husband planted the garden at Moonlight Cottage) and she still lives at Rose Hill, a few miles away. 'At that time there were quite a few of them roaming about,' she says. 'I heard the roar of a tiger one evening at the back. I was cutting flowers. I ran down and told one of my men. We saw the paw marks all over the cabbage bed the next morning. At that time the tigers were all going for dogs.'

So does she think Thompson was taken by a tiger? She shakes her head. 'He cannot be dead here, because after that they have the army people, the soldiers, the *orang asli* [forest tribesmen], all trying to find him for days, you see. They know the jungle very well. Even if he has been eaten by a tiger there must be some trace, or clothing, or something left behind.'

In the Highlands the 'lost in the jungle' theory seems less

sensible than it did in Bangkok. It is not even certain that he went into the jungle at all. He was a smoker, but when he walked down the drive at Moonlight he left his cigarettes and lighter. Nor did he take the pills which he carried in case of a gallstone attack. His silver pill-box, jokingly called his 'jungle box', was still in his room. About three hours of daylight remained when he set out. If either of the later sightings is genuine, he had still not gone into the jungle by 4 pm, with only two hours of light left.

From the look of it, at least, Thompson had neither the intention to go very far into the jungle, nor the time to do so. If he did go into the jungle, and something happened to him—a tiger, a snake bite, 'killer bees', a heart attack, a fall into an illicit animal trap, a poisoned aboriginal dart, all of which have been mooted—he must still have been fairly close to Moonlight or to one of those other bungalows when it happened. In these areas, naturally, the search was most intense, but turned up nothing.

BACK IN Bangkok I heard about an Englishman known as 'Major David'. I was told that he was ex-SAS, ran a Mexican restaurant on Patpong Road, and had been involved in the search for Thompson. As it turned out, he was actually ex-Ghurkas, and when I finally met him, it was in a Pakistani restaurant in Manila, but the important part of the information was true.

David Shaw (Major, retd) is a laconic character with an eye

that sizes you up. I was early for the appointment, but he was already there. He describes himself as a 'security consultant'. His clients include foreign companies setting up in Manila, and Filipino armed forces, both national and private. He is still in the business of jungle survival, he jokes, only now the jungle is Manila.

In March 1967, the men of the 2nd Battalion Second Ghurka Rifles were on cool-climate R & R in the Cameron Highlands after a ten-month stint 'killing Indonesian Communists in Borneo'. Among them was Shaw, then a lieutenant. When Thompson went missing, the Ghurkas formed a search party and Shaw, as the battalion Intelligence Officer—'the shit at the end of the line'—was put in charge of it. They began their search on Tuesday morning, some 36 hours after the first alarm. It involved two companies, about 300 men, and Shaw insists it was very thorough.

'We swept the whole area,' he says. 'This wasn't a question of following tracks, because in military terminology you never walk along tracks in the jungle anyway. We were making straight-line sweeps along a ridge-side, then the other side, then checking back to the road. Using the bungalow as a centre, I would say we probably did a mile all round, maybe a mile and a half, which is a lot of ground in the jungle. And there was nothing. We followed a lot of tracks but there was nothing that looked anything to do with a white male. We turned up a baby, dead, and we turned up some tiger tracks, but the tiger was not dragging anything. Thompson was quite a big man. There would have been marks, there would have been blood.'

They searched for a week. Shaw is convinced that Thompson was not there, and pretty certain he never had been. 'This was a very high-calibre search party. The people we were using were excellent trackers. If we couldn't find anything in that area, there wasn't anything in that area.'

This is just one more opinion. It is based on first-hand experience, though there may also be an element of self-justification in it. But Shaw had something more to say, an 'impression' he had. He leant across the table, dropped his voice below the wail of Islamic musak. 'I thought the whole thing was very shady,' he said.

In what way shady?

'Well, we were the only ones who took any real sort of interest. The effort put into the search by the Malays was pretty weak. The PFF [Police Field Force] came up, and they brought in some aboriginal trackers, but we thought they did a very half-hearted job.'

Was this, I asked, just a matter of laziness. 'I doubt it. The PFF were the best of the Malaysian groups. I've worked with them; I've trained some of them. These were professionals. They weren't like the military, they didn't have a colonel who was in charge purely because he was a younger sultan's younger brother. So I would doubt it was idleness. If it had been the Malaysian army, yes I would have said so, but not the PFF.'

So why weren't they looking?

'My personal feeling is that they *knew* he wasn't there, and they were just putting up a bit of front. I feel very strongly, from the attitude of people involved, that somebody up there knew what had happened. There was very little positive action taken by the Malays. The Americans made a bit of noise too, but it was all show. That can only lead to speculation, especially with the guy being what he was: a leading builder of a Third World industry, an international figure.

'It was weird. It was very weird.'

Another man with interesting memories of the search for Thompson is David Fitzstevens, a tall, red-bearded American who works for CAMA Services Inc, a Protestant aid organisation running projects in Vietnam, Laos and Cambodia.

In 1967 Fitzstevens was a sixteen-year-old student at the Dalat Missionary School, which had recently transferred to the Cameron Highlands from Vietnam. On the Monday morning, the day after Thompson's disappearance, the headmaster asked for volunteers to join the search party, and Fitzstevens was one of them.

At about midday, he and a friend were working through dense foliage in the woods below the back of Moonlight Cottage. He estimates it was about 50 metres from the house. 'We were coming up a slope, and there was this tree with big roots sticking out where the soil had eroded away, and something caught my eye. I shone my flashlight in there, and saw this small, bright, white object. It was some gauze, stuffed into the roots. It was very new, and it was very white. That's why I saw it. It couldn't have been there for long.'

He fished it out carefully. To a sixteen-year-old versed in Hollywood cop movies the implications were obvious. Thompson was a target for a kidnap gang; kidnappers used chloroform; here was a wad of gauze hastily hidden near the scene of the crime. At the least it showed that someone had recently been lurking in that area of jungle where there were no paths and no tracks, nothing at all except Moonlight Cottage 50 metres away, where Thompson was staying.

Excited by his discovery, Fitzstevens hurried back to Moonlight, where the local police had set up their headquarters. He found their reaction 'strange'. 'It was a kind of neutral response. They just said, "Well, thank you very much." I think they stuck it in a plastic bag. It was played down, a thing of no importance. And it's odd, but it seemed there was a relationship: after we'd turned this in, they moved us to another area entirely, a long way away.'

It is also odd, Fitzstevens thinks, that in all the sifting of the case that has gone on since, no one has made any reference to his discovery. There is nothing about it in the press reports, nor in the reminiscences of Connie Mangskau and the Lings, nor in Warren's biography. 'I've been waiting for 25 years for someone to mention it,' he says.

There may, of course, be some innocent explanation for the gauze—a hunter cleaning his gun, perhaps—but you wonder what else might have turned up, during the search or later, which the investigators decided not to mention.

NEITHER SHAW nor Fitzstevens has been interviewed before. They have no recollection of one another. Quite independently they raise these questions about the investigation of

Thompson's disappearance. The search was only for 'show', according to Shaw, and at least one possible clue in this clueless puzzle was quietly ignored. And so suspicion steals back into one's mind, and one starts to shuffle once more through the deck of conspiracy theories.

The earliest, and perhaps most interesting, was the 'Pridi connection', which linked Thompson with a former Thai Prime Minister, General Pridi Panyomyang. It is interesting because it was advanced by a top-brass soldier—General Edwin Black, Commander-in-chief of US forces in Thailand.

Black is now dead, but his views were outlined for me by his (and Thompson's) friend Maxine North in the office of her company, Starwagon Holdings, in Bangkok's business district. 'Ed's theory,' she explained, 'was that Jim had been approached by Pridi's people, his "young Turks" as we called them. They were planning to stage a coup and install Pridi again. They wanted to know how the US government would react to this, and reckoned Jim should be able to gauge this.' In the Cameron Highlands, Thompson was spirited away to meet Pridi. Whether he went willingly to this rendezvous, or was abducted, is a variable in the theory.

There is certainly some foundation for this. Thompson had been a friend of Pridi's, who led the 'Free Thai' resistance against the Japanese during the Second World War, and he was personally involved in the post-war power struggle between Pridi and his rival, Luang Pibul Songgram. In 1947 Pridi was ousted in a coup. Two years later he led an unsuccessful counter-coup. In the aftermath of this, three of Thompson's

closest Thai friends—all former members of the Pridi government—were murdered in police custody, and his chief assistant
in the silk business, a Laotian named Tao Oum, fled the country in fear of his life. This was, says Warren, a time of 'horror'
for Thompson: his best Asian friends killed or imprisoned or
driven into exile on charges which he believed to be untrue.

Pridi sought refuge in China. He disappeared from view
behind the Bamboo Curtain in the mid-Sixties, believed to be
based in Canton. According to the Thai government, he was
behind the Communist insurgents then active in southern
Thailand. In July 1968, a senior Thai official on a visit to Malaysia named Pridi as an 'architect of the Communist underground movement' in both Thailand and Malaysia. North and
east of the Cameron Highlands the jungle stretches unbroken
to the Thai border. This was the domain of the Communist
guerrillas. If someone wanted to meet up with Pridi, a remote
cottage in the Highlands might be a convenient rendezvous.

Apart from the customary lack of evidence, the Pridi theory
has problems. Thompson's known links with the Pridi faction,
says Warren, were 'strong in the late Forties, maybe in the early
Fifties, but certainly not by the Sixties. They were all long since
gone by that time. People have a way, when they're talking
about Jim, of sort of telescoping things that took place years
apart.' Of General Black, Warren says, in his deadpan way, 'Ed
was a nice man. He wasn't very bright, but he was a nice man.'

Nor does the theory explain why Thompson never came
back. Maxine North's version—'Jim knew too much [about
Pridi's plans], so they had to keep him'—is rather crude. In his

last years, which he spent in Paris, Pridi denied any knowledge of Thompson's fate, but then—to borrow a phrase from another cause célèbre of the Sixties—he would, wouldn't he?

THE BOTTOM line of the Pridi theory, and of other political theories that have been advanced, is another question: Was Thompson working for the CIA?

He certainly had the pedigree. During the war he was in the OSS (the Office of Strategic Services, the military intelligence wing which was a direct forbear of the CIA), and was briefly US Consul in Bangkok. He was pre-eminently a man of contacts. On the one hand, he was in close social contact with military figures such as General Black and with CIA station chief Bob Jantsen. On the other hand, he personally knew and admired the North Vietnamese leader, Ho Chi Minh, and had old friends from the silk business who belonged to Laotian nationalist groups. This is a kind of fulcrum for covert political work. Maxine North, the doyenne of the conspiracy theorists, has no doubt: 'The CIA knew who he was going to meet down there.'

Warren argues, predictably but cogently, that Thompson did not have time to be a spy. 'I've known a lot of spies, because Bangkok is—used to be—quite full of them. But there was never much doubt who was. There rarely is, in a place like this.'

Perhaps the best ones are the ones you *don't* know about?

'I doubt if there were many you didn't know about, frankly. I really and truly do.'

I later spoke to Don Carmichael, who knew Thompson in Bangkok in the Fifties. Carmichael was himself described to me as ex-CIA, though he denies this. He was, he says, 'a straight airline guy,' though the airline in question was Civil Air Transport, the forerunner of Air America. This was put together by General Chenault in the early Fifties as a supply-line to the KMT (the anti-Communist Kuomintang) holed up in Burma. The operation, it is now well known, also involved shipping large quantities of opium out of the KMT's fiefdom.

Carmichael had, as he puts it, 'administrative status' in the outfit. He was later a 'consultant' in Washington for the US Department of Defence, and now runs a real estate business in Florida. I asked this 'straight airline guy', by telephone, whether Thompson had worked for the CIA. It depends, he said, what you mean by 'worked for'. 'I doubt if Jim was an agent, but 99 chances out of 100 he was a contact for the US intelligence people in Bangkok. He was a terribly knowledge-able man, with high-ranking contacts. He had contacts in Phnom Penh. He was certainly an intelligence asset. He didn't need the money, but he was a patriotic man.'

Much the same view is taken by Barrie Cross, an associate of Thompson's in the Oriental Hotel and the son-in-law of Connie Mangskau. 'Jim was Sea-Supply, which was the fore-runner of the CIA, there's no doubt about that. I think it's true to say that once you're a member of a covert organisation you can never really leave. I'm sure they consulted him. He was very aware politically. He knew what was going on.'

The veteran Indo-China reporter Alan Dawson introduces

yet another twist. Like some other OSS veterans, he claims, Thompson had actually been rejected by the CIA. He was 'generally believed to be a secret agent', and both he and the CIA went along with this 'because it took the heat off the *real* agents in Bangkok'.

SO ONE throws up the pieces and lets them land in another pattern of reminiscence and rumour. It could all fit into one superb, gold-plated conspiracy theory—the restlessness at the picnic as the meeting drew near; the sightings at the bungalows, which afford a clearer view of the road below than you get from Moonlight Cottage; the curious impressions of both Shaw and Fitzstevens that the search they took part in was more of a cover-up than a genuine search. This was 1967, the first flush of the Vietnam War. We now know something of what was going on behind the scenes: the missionary-spies working out of up-country Thailand, the clandestine wooing of tribal armies, the Air America opium-moves, the ground plans for the 'Secret War' in Laos and Cambodia. These contexts seem to legitimise a conspiracy theory: the maverick Pridi is only one possibility.

Thompson lives on in this limbo. You come to know the man a little, and to like him rather a lot: 'a curious, imaginative, engrossing, sometimes lonely man, who chose an unlikely course for his life.' People speak of him in a relaxed, anecdotal way; they enjoy telling the story, for the hundredth time—'So I called Jim up . . .', 'Jim always used to say . . .', Jim with his creased silk trousers and his beer belly, Jim driving down a tree-lined street in his convertible, Jim clowning it up with his cockatoo, Cocky, Jim getting red in the face when he ate *thom yam kung* soup. I was surprised to learn from Nath Chaijaroen that he never mastered the Thai language: 'He used to say his tongue was not soft enough.'

In some of his friends there is a desire to let his bones rest in some sequestered niche of the Cameron Highlands. In others there is an opposite wish: to keep scratching away for a story they believe has not yet been told. After 25 years the case remains unresolved and somehow spooky, as if we were all still waiting for him to saunter back up the drive in time for a sundowner.

the capital of memory

THE **GLORIES** of Alexandria are past and gone, but that has been the case for nearly two millennia now, and I doubt I'm the first visitor to feel a touch of disappointment on arriving. It is now a major metropolis: Egypt's second city. Coming in on the bus from Cairo—three hours up the Desert Highway, brain numbed by Egyptian soaps on the video—you see it sprawled like a long grubby mirage along a strip of land between the Mediterranean and the polluted marshes of Lake Mariout. The population is officially four million, but is almost certainly nearer five. It is not as crowded and traffic-ridden as Cairo, and the sea is always just a few blocks away, but if you

Mail on Sunday, 1996

are looking for tranquil reveries of ancient history you will look in vain in downtown Alexandria.

Though the glories are gone, much of the city's charm still remains. It is a curious, slightly seedy charm, not easy to discern at first, and not easy to define thereafter. The British novelist Lawrence Durrell, who lived here for years, speaks of 'glimpsing the phantom city' which lies somewhere behind the ramshackle modern façade.

I had a reservation at the Metropole Hotel. I was looking for 'character', and the Metropole, I was assured, had bags of it. A dowdy neo-classical building with thin balconies and tall shutters, it once housed the semi-legendary Office of the Third Circle of Irrigation, where the eccentric Alexandrian poet Constantine Cavafy earned his living for more than 30 years. Among his acquaintances was another literary visitor, E. M. Forster, who wrote: 'You turn and see a Greek gentleman in a straw hat, standing absolutely motionless at a slight angle to the universe: it is Mr Cavafy.' He is on his way to the office, however, and 'vanishes with a slight gesture of despair'.

In 1934 the building was converted into a hotel, Greek-owned, with lavish Art Deco salons on the first floor. It sounded the classic Alexandrian spot: lashings of faded grandeur and a literary ghost or two.

No more, however: disappointment again. As I checked in I could hear ominous sounds of drilling. The Metropole has changed hands, refurbishment is under way, and soon, the elderly lift man tells me, it will be *tout nouveau*. Much the same has already happened to the city's most famous hotel, the Cecil, now owned by the Sofitel chain.

We ascended slowly in the lift, a wood-panelled kiosk about the size of a wardrobe. I had a seaview room on the fourth floor. Refurbishment had not reached there yet. The room was huge and sombre, and resonated to the noise of the tram terminus and coach station of Saad Zaghlul Square below, but as I threw back the shutters and took in the view—the westward curve of the bay along the Corniche, the ageing Italian-built apartment houses, the clouds massing behind the minarets of the Abdulkadir el Shorbagy mosque—my heart lifted.

THE CITY was founded by Alexander the Great in 332 BC. His body lies somewhere beneath the city, probably around the busy junction of Al Horreya and Nabi Daniel Streets. No one is sure.

In classical times it was famed for its lighthouse, the Pharos (one of the Seven Wonders of the Ancient World); for its immense library containing some 500,000 manuscripts; and for its seductive Queen Cleopatra the Fifth. In the square below the Metropole stood the Caesareum, an enormous temple begun by Cleopatra in about 40 BC. This crumbled away long ago, but one of the granite obelisks which adorned it remained here until 1887, when it was taken to London. It is now 'Cleopatra's Needle' on the Thames Embankment.

But this is only the bottom layer of Alexandrian history. The city's position on the Mediterranean has made it a crossroads of Greek, Turkish, Arab and European influences, and has brought it the chequered history and louche, cosmopolitan air which Lawrence Durrell captures so richly in the *Alexandria Quartet*.

It is literally a city of layers. The city's topography is restrictive: the central area—hemmed in between the sea, desert and lake—has been constantly rebuilt. As the pace of new building accelerates, the archaeologists struggle to keep up. One morning I accompanied the eminent Alexandrian scholar Professor Mustafa Abbadi to see the latest find. On the way he reminisced about his days as a student at Cambridge in the Fifties. When they asked him where he had learned to row so well, he told them: 'On the Nile!' We are visiting the site of one of the city's old picture-palaces, the Cinema Diane, recently demolished. Beneath it they have found a 2nd-century Roman villa, with cisterns and wells, and on its dining-room floor an exquisite, sexy mosaic of the Medusa. The young archaeologist pulls off the polythene tarpaulin, dusts her lightly with water. She glowers dangerously like those *femmes fatales* who flickered across the cinema screen above her. Her eyes are looking sideways, so she didn't turn the guests to stone when they walked in to dinner.

Down along the Corniche, a more ambitious rescue is under way. Two years ago, a team of divers under the flamboyant French archaeologist Jean-Yves Empéreur started bringing up pieces of the Pharos itself. Built in the 3rd-century BC, this immense lighthouse stood more than 400 feet tall and looked a little like the Empire State Building. Its beam was a fire magnified by mirrors or lenses, and fed (it is thought) by a fleet of donkeys carrying firewood up a spiral staircase.

The Pharos was destroyed by a series of earthquakes, and lies scattered over five acres of seabed below the headland. The divers have recovered Ptolemaic statues, parts of a sphinx, and one immense, 75-ton slab of granite and marble, which was probably part of the parapet on the first floor of the lighthouse. Many of the statues turn out to have been brought from Heliopolis, the Pharaonic city near Cairo.

'Things do not change,' says Empéreur with a shrug. 'In the 3rd-century BC it was very *à la mode* to bring Pharaonic statues here, just as it was in the 19th-century to take them to Paris or London.'

DURRELL CALLED Alexandria 'the capital of memory', a place where the past is always in the air, 'clinging to the minds of old men like traces of perfume upon a sleeve'.

Only fragments remain of Classical Alexandria, but its more recent past can be savoured just by wandering aimlessly through the streets, past shabby villas and rococo facades and dusty bric-a-brac shops. The city seems like an ageing dandy fallen on hard times. Lingering over a café creme under the improbable chandeliers of the Trianon, or taking a lunchtime aperitif at the marble-topped bar of the Cap d'Or, it is easy to imagine yourself back in the Alexandria of Forster and Cavafy: a strange backwater of classicism and poetry and sexual adventure.

Forster came here during the Great War as a Red Cross worker. He was in his mid-thirties, a small, bespectacled man, already famous for novels like *Howards End* and *A Room With A View*. Here he fell in love with a local tram conductor, Mohammed el Adl, and haunted the terminus below the Metropole. They quarrelled over a box of cakes. Mohammed's death, in 1922, devastated Forster. Cavafy was also homosexual, and many of his finest poems are about the boys he picked up in the billiard halls and brothels of Tatwig Street. Forster wrote a superb guide-book to Alexandria. Printed here privately in 1922, it is still the best guide to the Classical vestiges of the city. The first edition is rare because almost all the copies were destroyed in a fire.

The English have a long association with 'Alex'. For families working here during the British occupation of Egypt it was the summer bolt-hole from Cairo, an expat scene which Durrell summed up acidly as 'boredom laced with drink and Packards and beach cabins'.

Durrell, brother of naturalist Gerald, came here in the Forties. His house can still be seen—just. You walk across the railtracks, down Suez Canal Street and into the narrow streets of a residential quarter called Moharren Bey. You see the tower first, dark sandstone, suggestive of a minor English manor house. The house is boarded up. The watchmen are under instructions to let no one in, and I wouldn't for a moment suggest they were open to backsheesh. The villa stands amid its rampant shrubbery like a forgotten folly. There is a walled garden with ancient fruit trees, and the remains of a stable, and washing strung across the porch. It is just an old address in the 'capital of memory'.

Actual memories of the old cosmopolitan Alexandria are fading fast, but not quite gone. At the Elite restaurant Madame Kristina holds court behind the cash register. She is Greek, an ageless, matriarchal figure in the large Greek community. 'But one of my grandmothers was Austrian,' she adds coquettishly, 'which is why I am so blonde.'

Her father was an immigrant shopkeeper; as a child she met Cavafy; she remembers the day Edith Piaf dined at the Elite. Even today it has a faded *fin de siècle* air, with its old French theatre posters and dusty check tablecloths. Does she think Alexandria was better in the old days? '*Mais oui!*' (Like many in this mongrel city she speaks several languages, sometimes in the same sentence.) 'But I have lived here so long, there is nowhere else to go.'

THE CURRENT fate of Durrell's house is typical of the battle now being waged for the architectural heart and soul of the city. On one side its owners, an Italian family called Ambron, intent on redevelopment; and on the other side, a local architect, Mohammed Awad, the president of the Alexandrian Preservation Trust. 'We have to battle,' he tells me. 'The old houses are just seen as cumbersome old structures that should be cleared away.'

It is often a losing battle. The billiard halls where Cavafy cruised have gone. The villas and picture palaces are coming down, and the Cecil Hotel is a glum parody of itself. This was once *the* hotel in Alex, and during the Desert War the upstairs bar served as an impromptu HQ for General Montgomery. You can still take a sundowner in Monty's Bar but don't expect any kind of atmosphere—even the Mona Lisa, in lurid repro in the corner, seems to be waiting for you to leave.

But in the end it isn't just the architecture that gives the place its peculiar evocative charm. More, it is the people; and most it is an atmosphere, a mood as elusive as the aromatic, peachy smoke that wafts out of the hubble-bubble cafés. As the old man at the Metropole said: 'Soon it will be *tout nouveau.*' He sounds neither pleased nor regretful about it. Things change, but in the capital of memory, the past is always there to catch you unawares.

legless in mexico

MALCOLM LOWRY died 40 years ago this month, his stomach full of gin and barbiturates, his body ravaged by chronic alcoholism. He was 47 years old. The coroner recorded a verdict of misadventure; there were unconfirmed whispers of suicide.

Lowry died in a rented cottage in Sussex, but his name is indelibly associated with Mexico, the setting of his masterpiece, *Under the Volcano*. The book was first published in 1947, so this is really a double-anniversary year for Lowry. It seemed an auspicious time to go off in search of 'Lowry's Mexico'.

The trail begins in the pleasant town of Cuernavaca, an hour's drive south of Mexico City. To be more precise, it

Independent on Sunday, 1997

begins on a certain concrete bollard on a street called Calle Rio Balsas. If you stand on this, on tiptoe, you can just see over the wall opposite, to a large pinkish-coloured building set in overgrown gardens. It used to be a hotel called the Casino de la Selva.

Among the trees is a statue of the conquistador Hernan Cortés, whom Keats famously imagined standing 'silent upon a peak in Darien', staring at the Pacific, though it was in fact the less scannable Nuñez de Balboa who did that. But my eye is fixed on the old hotel, and in particular the balconied terrace which runs along the front of it at first-floor level. It is the precise spot where *Under the Volcano* begins.

'Towards sunset on the Day of the Dead in November 1939, two men in white flannels sat on the main terrace of the Casino drinking anis . . .'

The two men are Dr Vigil and Jacques Laruelle. The scene is a kind of prologue to the main action, which describes the last day in the life of the ex-Consul, Geoffrey Firmin. The volcano of the title is the great mountain Popocatapetl, which in those pollution-free days could be clearly seen from here. Lowry's drinking buddy, the American poet Conrad Aiken, nicknamed the book 'Poppa-gets-the-botl'.

I had imagined taking a commemorative anis on the terrace, but it was not to be. The hotel closed down a couple of years ago. As the cigarette-seller standing nearby puts it simply: *'No existe.'* There is an ostentatiously padlocked gate. There is a nightclub called Mambo, also closed, in what was probably one of the hotel's outbuildings. And there is the Happy Vally (*sic*) parking-lot, with its logo of a top hat tipped vaguely towards the hotel's former identity as a casino, though this was already in the past when Lowry was here. 'It is no a longer a casino,' he wrote. 'You cannot even dice for drinks in the bar.'

I have tried to get a closer look, but the Happy Vally security guard won't let me into the parking-lot without a ticket, so I must be content with this distant viewpoint, silent upon a bollard in Cuernavaca, and with the friendly cigarette-seller as my chief informant. 'It was a fine hotel,' he says. 'It had more than 300 rooms. Very de luxe.'

Among the lollipops and tortilla crisps and 'I Love Mexico' cigarette-lighters on his stall, he finds an old post-card of the hotel, but all it shows is the hotel's swimming pool, with some old-fashioned deck-chairs and a couple of waistcoated waiters. I buy it anyway. The pickings are slim, but that is the nature of these literary pilgrimages.

LOWRY ARRIVED in Cuernavaca in late 1936, with his first wife Jan (Yvonne in *Under the Volcano*). He was 27 years old, the black-sheep son of a wealthy Cheshire industrialist, a published novelist (*Ultramarine*, 1933), a former merchant-seaman, a 'two fisted drinker', a literary drifter.

Photographs of him at this time make him look like a dodgy prep school master—the pipe, the beard, the shock of hair, the tweedy trousers. Conrad Aiken describes him, in the summer of 1937, in the *zócalo* or plaza of Cuernavaca: 'the slightly absurd but always altogether delightful figure advancing towards them; his trousers knotted round the waist with a necktie, and looking as if they might fall off any minute; and grinning at them shyly and affectionately and a little drunkenly.'

Cuernavaca must have been a charming place then. It still is, though the population, a mere 8,000 in Lowry's day, is now over half a million. The Aztecs called it Quauhnahuac, 'on the edge of the woods'. The Spanish garbled this to Cuernavaca, meaning 'cow-horn'. Lowry used the older, uncompromised spelling.

At an altitude of 5,000 ft, lushly fertile, and blessed with the 'eternal spring' of the *tierra templada*, Cuernavaca is a popular weekend resort from Mexico City, with secretive high-walled villas in the burgeoning suburbs. It has always been a place of recreation, retirement and comfortable exile. The Aztec nobility summered here; Cortés followed suit and built his rather grim palace. It was the favourite retreat of Maximilian, the melancholy Austro-Hungarian prince who reigned briefly as Emperor of Mexico in the 1860s, and his young wife Charlotte or Carlotta. Maximilian fell for a local Indian girl, and built a well-appointed love-nest in the village of Acapatzingo, now a sleepy suburb.

'Cuernavaca is a city of ghosts,' says Ruth Davidoff, a long-time resident of the town. 'We live among them.' (Her own ghost even, she adds, for behind her on the mantelpiece is her portrait, painted 50 years ago by Diego Rivera.)

At one time or another the town has been home to exiles like the Shah of Iran and Papa Doc Duvalier and Maria José, the last Queen of Italy. The screen actress Helen Hayes had a house here, as did the millionairess Barbara Hutton. Here Charles Lindbergh met his wife Anne, daughter of the American financier Dwight Morrow, who was US ambassador to Mexico in the 1920s.

And here, in this bougainvillea-bowered hideaway, in this 'sunny place for shady people', with a verandah on Calle Humboldt to sit and write on, and an allowance of $100 a month from his father to live on, and a young and very beautiful wife—in short, one may say tut-tuttingly, with everything apparently going for him—here Lowry fell into the black spiral of drunkenness, jealousy and despair which he chronicles with such alarming honesty in *Under the Volcano*.

After the locked-up casino, there is further disappointment on Calle Humboldt. It does not seem possible to locate the house in which Lowry lived, and where he began the first draft of *Volcano*. The street numbers have changed many times, the last time recently enough for most houses to carry two numbers. Lowry's own evidence is contradictory: his letters are written from Calle Humboldt 62, but he later refers to their former home as No. 15.

It was not the building at the top of the street which is now the Hotel Bajo el Volcán—the only visible allusion to Lowry that I found in the whole town. The manageress, Señora Avila Tellez, assures me he lived here, but it is actually the house he gives to the adulterous Frenchman Laruelle in *Under the Volcano*. Its characteristic twin-towers can be seen, though later

additions obscure them. The consul's house—Lowry's house—
was lower down the street, and single storey.

The cinema on Morelos Street is still there: in the book it
was showing *The Hands of Orlac* with Peter Lorre. So is the
penitentiary, now euphemistically described as the Centro Es-
tatal de Readaptácion Social. And there are the *barrancas,* the
steep, rubbish-choked ravines which cut through the town like
ugly scars, and which in Lowry's Dantesque imagination become a glimpse of hell—'vast, threatening, gloomy, dark,
frightening: the terrific drop, the darkness below.'

And what of Charlie's Bar? None of the elderly residents I
spoke to seemed to recall it. It was his favourite watering hole,
with its 'throbbing refrigerator' and its 'upturned spittoons'. A
letter to Conrad Aiken ends: 'Come to Charlie's, where I am,
soon: old Aggie's got the orrors something orful'.

In his memoirs Aiken recalls their marathon binges at Charlie's—'the drunken words competing with the uproar of the
square, the barking of maimed dogs, the mad bicyclists, the
busses roaring in and out, and that demonic bird in the café
next door . . .'

A snatch of conversation goes thus:

'Have another tequila?'

'Yes, how I hate the bloody stuff. Charlie! And these bloody
little limes. And good jumping Christ, there's that bitch again,
and that bloody bird . . .'

'Well, here's to death and betrayal. Mine first, yours after-
ward.'

Aiken describes Charlie's as 'a little corner café with open stone arches and red covered tables, facing the palace square'. After diligent enquiry, I believe it was the bar now called Flash Flaco. This was formerly called the Tequila Roja; before that, in the early 1980s, El Mostachio de Pepe: further back than that I cannot get. It fits Aiken's description geographically, and is the first bar you would come to on the 'palace square'—the Alameda—if you were coming up, thirstily, from Calle Humboldt.

They would not recognise it now: the bland international decor, the piped rock-musak, the video screen showing some kind of Mexican MTV, the sushi bar. It is fun tracking these places down—I sometimes suspect the lingering influence of Big Chief I-Spy: one is 'spotting' literary backdrops as one used to spot green woodpeckers and Westmoreland terriers—but the reality is so often disappointing. You are, quite simply, in the right place at the wrong time.

And so you wind up, after a day of enjoyable but pointless pursuit, in the crowded *zócalo* to which all roads lead. It is the evening hour they call *entre dos luces,* between two lights; the hour of strollers and talkers observing the day's departure; the hour one is quietly in love with Mexico. The *urraccas,* the small glossy crows of the region, are making a phenomenal racket in the trees, exactly as Lowry heard them—'shatterers of the twilight hour . . . the *zócalo* rings with their incessant drilling mechanic screech'. And suddenly, amid this twilight hubbub, you begin to place him. He would come shambling purposefully across the square, past the bandstand with its cramped arcade of juice-stalls underneath, past the corn-cob cooks, and the balloon-sellers with their great floating bouquets, and the shoeshine customers in their little canopied thrones, this 'carelessly powerful' but 'slightly absurd' figure advancing towards you.

And you wonder: would you be glad to see him, or would you slip off into the crowd to avoid him?

On balance, probably the former, the drunkenness redeemed by his humour, his learning, his 'wonderful visionary gift of the gab.' His friend David Markson said: 'Time with Lowry was somehow concentrated, distilled.' Another long-suffering acquaintance said: 'Just one look at the old bastard makes me happy for a week.'

THOUGH LOWRY lived mostly in Cuernavaca, he also drew deeply on the handsome, airy town of Oaxaca (pronounced 'wahaca') in southwestern Mexico. He stayed at the Hotel Francia, which is still in business—there are the stairs down which he would creep at night, past the sleeping porter, to crawl the cantinas until dawn with his Zapotec Indian friend, Juan Fernando Márquez, the model for Dr Vigil. He visited the shrine of Nuestra Señora de la Soledad, which Márquez (and Vigil) called the church 'for those who have nobody with'.

He came here after splitting up with Jan: he was on the skids. 'Oaxaca! The word was like a breaking heart, a sudden peal of stifled bells in a gale . . .' He was several times 'clapped in the local chokey', as he puts it, for being drunk and for expressing unpopular anti-Fascist views. 'In a Mexican prison you have to drink out of a piss pot sometimes, especially when you have no passport'.

By a marvellous twist, the gaol which housed Lowry for some weeks over Christmas 1937-8, and on other occasions, is now Oaxaca's most luxurious hotel, the Camino Real. Originally a convent, it was expropriated in 1862 by the reformist government of Benito Juarez, and served as the municipal prison till 1976. In a secluded courtyard there is a doorway scrawled with prisoners' graffiti. One reads: 'in this cursed prison where poverty reigns we are punished for our crime and also for our poverty'. Another says simply, *'No Hay Libertad'*. There is no freedom.

In Oaxaca I concluded—or admitted what I had known all along—that if Lowry's ghost was to be found anywhere, it was at the bottom of a bottle of mescal. In his fragmentary novel-cum-memoir, *Dark as the Grave Wherein my Friend is Laid,* Lowry writes eloquently in praise of this Mexican fire-water: it is a 'pure drink', a 'civilised drink', though also a dangerously powerful one—'The evils that dwell in rye dwell not in it, though others, worse, may . . . In mescal lies the principle of that god-like or daemonic force in Mexico that, anyone who has lived there knows, remains to this day unappeased.'

Mexico produces 8 million litres of mescal a year and three out every four is produced in the Oaxaca region. If you need to get legless in Mexico, this is the place to do it. Half an hour out of Oaxaca, on the road between Tlacolula and Mitla, you come to a low building with a sign saying FABRICA DE MESCAL. It has more the look of a farmstead than a factory, its outbuildings merging into sparse scrub. The plain is dotted with large spiky plants that have a spray of spear-like leaves. These are the blue agave, or aloe, known as *maguey*—the raw material of what you are repeatedly told is the best mescal in the world.

Five men stand in the interior gloom, round the still, talking softly and drinking. The still is formed of a metal tank of hot water and a smaller cylinder, called the *olla,* or stewpot, which contains the fermented maguey. They courteously show me round. Here is the earthen oven in which the maguey is cooked; it emerges a dull, sodden orange colour, like a giant rhubarb, and has at this point a sweet, caramelish taste when chewed. Here is the 800 kg millstone, and the mule which pulls it, and the vats in which the mash is distilled for three days. And then they invite me to drink.

There are various forms of mescal and after an hour of concentrated Mexican hospitality, I have sampled just about all of them. The best known is *mescal de gusano.* The *gusano* is a grub which inhabits the maguey: a specimen floats pickled in the bottle, to be swallowed by the last-drop drinker who derives all sorts of powers thereby. (For export to Taiwan, they put three or four *gusanos* in the bottle.) There is *mescal de pechuga,* or 'chicken-breast mescal', so-called for the slice of maguey leaf floating in it, imparting a pretty honey-colour to the brew. There are flavoured mescals—orange, camomile, almond— and vintage mescals aged up to 10 years in oak barrels. And there is the pure, colourless, unsullied *mescal del monte,* just as Nature intended.

It is indeed a wonderful drink, very pure—not even sugar is added, the natural sweetness of the maguey being sufficient— and seems to get you high more than drunk.

Night has fallen, the moon is up, the last bus to Oaxaca has long gone. The bottle goes round once more.

'*Salud y pesetas!*'

'*Y tiempo para gastarlas!*'

It is the traditional toast, as raised by Vigil and Laruelle on the terrace of the casino, and doubtless many times by Lowry himself: 'Health and wealth—and time to enjoy them'.

I drain the little cup of smoky-tasting mescal, the 'bloody stuff' that brought him none of these things, only moments of pure intoxication such as this, on the moonlit plains of Tlacolula, with the words of Dr Vigil seeming to whisper in my ear: 'Come, amigo, throw away your mind.'

conversing with giants

THERE ARE stories about giants in just about every lan-
guage in the world, but this one is different. The earliest
surviving version of it is found in manuscript copies, in both
French and Italian, dating from about 1523. It begins as follows:

One day, quite unexpectedly, we saw a giant. He was on the
shore of the sea, completely naked, dancing and leaping and
singing, and as he sang he poured sand and dust over his head.
The Captain sent one of the sailors over to him. He told the
sailor to sing and leap like the giant, so as to reassure him and
show him friendship. This the sailor did, and presently led the
giant to a little island where the Captain was waiting. When

Granta, 1998

the giant stood before us he began to be astonished and afraid, and he raised one finger upwards, thinking that we came from heaven. He was so tall that the tallest of us only came up to his waist, and his body was very well built. He had a large face painted red all over, and his eyes were painted yellow, and there were two hearts painted on his cheeks. He had only a little hair on his head; this was painted white. When he came before the Captain he had clothed himself in the skin of a certain beast, very skilfully sewed. This creature has the head and ears of a mule, a neck and body like a camel's, the legs of a deer, and the tail of a horse. There is a great quantity of these creatures here. The giant's feet were also covered with the skin of this animal, made into shoes. The Captain had food and drink brought to the giant, and then the men showed him some things, among them a steel mirror. When the giant saw his likeness in it, he was greatly terrified, and leaped backwards, and in doing so knocked down three or four of our men.

There are further incidents, to which I will return, but perhaps certain details have already suggested what is special about this story, what makes it different from Odysseus' encounter with the Cyclops or Jack's adventures up the beanstalk. For this is not a legend or a fairy tale; it is an encounter that occurred at a specific time and place, and was witnessed by several people besides the narrator. It is, in other words, a piece of travel writing. It belongs to a genre that might be called—to borrow the title of another 16th-century travel book—'News from the New World'. This does not necessarily dispose us to believe the story. Travel writers often exaggerate and sometimes lie, and when they have been at sea for nearly a year they might be expected to do both. Meeting a giant would certainly come under the heading of 'good copy', perhaps suspiciously so.

What interests me is precisely the ambiguity of the story. It is a true report that sounds like a fairy tale; it is a fairy tale that real people have experienced.

THE AUTHOR of this account was a young Italian gentleman called Antonio Pigafetta: an unsung hero of early sea travel. He was a member of the expedition commanded by the Portuguese adventurer Fernão de Magalhães, better known as Magellan. The expedition became famous for achieving the first circumnavigation of the world. The incident he was describing took place around the beginning of June 1520, on the coast of what is now Argentina. Magellan himself is the 'Captain' referred to in Pigafetta's account.

Little is known of Pigafetta's early life. He was born in the northern Italian town of Vicenza, probably in the year 1486. He may have seen some military service against the Turks— he compares the arrows of the 'giant' to Turkish arrows—but the first certain knowledge we have of him dates from early 1519, when he turned up in Barcelona in the service of another Vicentino, Monsignor Francesco Chiericati, a powerful churchman and politician who was then the *Protonotario* or Papal Ambassador to the court of the Spanish king, Charles V.

Here Pigafetta first learned of the 'small armada of five ships' being prepared by Magellan in Seville, and of its daring intention to sail not just to the New World of America, as others had done since the pioneering voyages of Columbus and Vespucci in the 1490s, but beyond it, in search of a new route to the spice-rich islands of the East Indies. He set off for Seville and signed up for the expedition.

He describes this decision with a mixture of awe and nonchalance: 'I knew the very great and awful things of the ocean, both from my reading of books and from conversing with certain learned and well-informed people who attended on my master the Protonotario. So now I determined to experiment, and to see with my own eyes some part of those things.'

In contemporary documents Pigafetta is described as *criado del capitán:* Magellan's aide or assistant. He is also described as a *sobresaliente,* or supernumerary. He was not, in other words, a regular member of the crew. He was not primarily a sailor at all, though he was a scholar of sorts, well-grounded in the mathematics and astronomy of the day (among his extant writings is a treatise on the computation of longitude). He was also a political servant, and was careful to note that he joined Magellan's expedition 'with the favour' of both his master the Protonotario and the Spanish king.

What these terms and contexts add up to is this: that Pigafetta was, probably for the first time on a voyage of this sort, specifically there in order to write about it. He was the observer, the chronicler, the reporter. His 'desire', and that of his masters, was 'that it might be said I had performed this voyage, and had seen well with my own eyes the things hereafter written'. The account he produced—drily entitled, in the French manuscript from which I am quoting, 'Navigation et Découvrement de la Indie Supérieure'—is mostly a fulfilment of this aim. It is lucid, factual, and demonstrably based on a journal or logbook kept throughout the voyage.

If his meeting with the 'giant' seems to us an exaggeration or a lie, it might not have been intended to be so. Was it something more like a hallucination, something so powerfully imagined that it seemed to be real?

THE MARINER bound for the New World faced many dangers. There were the tempests and twenty-foot waves of the Atlantic; the diseases and brutalities of life aboard ship; the threat of piracy or enemy action. There were the man-eating fish with teeth like saws which the Spanish sailors called *tiburón*. There were the periods of privation when men ate sawdust and oxhide, and dead rats fetched half a ducat apiece.

These, perhaps, were some of the 'great and awful things' envisaged by Antonio Pigafetta as he boarded Magellan's flagship, the *Trinidad*, in August 1519. Most of them he would come to experience in the course of his three-year journey round the world.

But no less pressing were the dangers of the imagination, the tricks of the mind, the visions that came when darkness fell and the sea was calm and he lay in his little cabin with his nostrils filled with the bonfire smoke of *estrenque*, the faggots of dried grass they burned on the poop as a beacon to the other vessels of the fleet, straggling along somewhere out there on the Ocean Sea.

For the ancient world, to which Pigafetta still partly belonged, the sea was a place peopled by apparitions: the sirens, mermaids, monsters and gods of classical mythology. In the Bible too the sea was associated with visions. 'They that go down to the sea in ships, that do business in great waters, these see the works of the Lord, and His wonders in the deep.'

These sea visions were elaborated into a darker idea of the 'deep' and its contents. St Augustine wrote: *'Mare saeculum est'*—the sea is the world, in other words, 'the element subject to the devil'. It is a 'gloomy abyss', the realm of power allotted to the devil and the demons after their fall. The impenetrable depths of the sea symbolize, indeed contain, the dark secrets of human sin. This is already some way towards the interpretations of modern psychoanalysis, in which the sea is thought of as a symbol or archetype of the unconscious. Jung refers to the visions associated with the sea as 'invasions by unconscious contents'.

To a man of learning like Pigafetta, this lent a magical dimension to that long and arduous sea-crossing, and some of it surfaced in his narrative. In the midst of a storm, he wrote:

The body of St Anselm appeared to us in the form of a fire lighted at the summit of the mainmast, and remained there near two hours and a half, which comforted us greatly, for we were in tears only expecting the hour of our perishing. And when that holy light was going away from us, it gave out such brilliance in our eyes that for nearly a quarter of an hour we were like people blinded and calling for mercy. It is to be noted that whenever that light which represents St Anselm shows itself and descends on a vessel in a storm at sea, that vessel is never lost. Immediately this light departed, the sea grew calmer, and then we saw various kinds of birds among which were some that had no fundament.

This was not a hallucination—he was describing the electrical phenomenon known as St Elmo's Fire—but the language tends towards the visionary, and ends with the rather inexplicable seabird that lacked (though how did he know?) an anus.

One has a sense of mental disorder here. Already the strange but true—'There are also fish that fly'—begins to mingle indistinguishably with the strange but not quite true. The grasp on what is possible grows weaker. And then, on St Lucy's Day, 13 December 1519, after nearly four months at sea, the fleet touched land on the coast of Brazil, and they were in the New World, where just about anything was possible.

AT FIRST, they were in territory already explored and marginally settled by Europeans. Some of the crew had been there before. They were careful to avoid the settlers, who were Portuguese (Magellan had deserted the Portuguese in favour of Spain, and his expedition was designed to break Portugal's monopoly of the East Indian spice-trade), but after the hazards of the crossing this was paradise. The climate was sweet, the land abundant, the natives amiable. They dined on tapir meat and 'a fruit named *battate* [sweet potato] which has the taste of chestnut and is the length of a shuttle'. A sense of relief and assurance is reflected in Pigafetta's text, which is busily observant at this point.

But as they moved slowly south, away from 'the equinoctial line', or equator, in search of the desired passage to the Pacific Ocean, they began to enter the kind of unknown landscape which is the real stuff of the New World experience.

Hic finis chartae viaeque: here ends the map, here ends the known way.

By the end of March 1520, more than four months after their first landfall, the fleet was coasting down along the grey, windwhipped tundra of what is now called Patagonia. They saw penguins, which Pigafetta called 'sea geese', and walrus ('sea wolves'). The weather was worsening, the companies were restless. Here, at a location which Pigafetta accurately estimated as 'forty nine degrees and a half in the Antarctic heavens' (i.e. 49 degrees 30 minutes South), they found shelter in a wide inlet which they christened Puerto San Julián, after the patron saint of hospitable welcome. They decided to winter here. For two months they saw no one at all. Then one day, around the beginning of June, 'quite unexpectedly', they met the giant.

LET US try and separate the elements of truth and fable in this encounter.

The 'giant' was almost certainly a Tehuelche or Tcheulchi, a member of one of the nomadic tribes of Patagonia. They were, and are, a very tall race. Bruce Chatwin described them as 'copperskinned hunters whose size, strength and deafening voices belied their docile character'. And that extraordinary hybrid creature of the region whose skins the giant wore—described by Pigafetta as part mule, part camel, part deer, and part horse—is also real. It is recognizably enough a guanaco, a smaller cousin of the llama still found in the area.

This much is true. The difficulty arises precisely with the use of the word 'giant'. This is not just a loose description, since Pigafetta specifically says that the tallest of the Europeans 'only came up to his waist'. Other members of the tribe are similarly perceived: they are all described as giants, and indeed giantesses—the latter's huge pendulous breasts are especially noted by Pigafetta. Nor is he alone in his perception of them. A fragmentary logbook kept by an unnamed Genoese mariner on the voyage says: 'There were people like savages, and the men were from nine to ten spans high.' A span, the width of an outstretched hand, is generally taken as nine inches: the giants were therefore reckoned by this observer to be as much as seven and a half feet tall.

This is certainly an overstatement, as later travellers were relieved but disappointed to find. In 1698 a French explorer, François Froger, wrote of 'the famous Patagons': 'Some authors avouch [them] to be eight or ten feet high. However, the tallest of them was not above six feet high.' The Guinness Book of Records states: 'The Tehuelche of Patagonia, long regarded as of gigantic stature (i.e. 7-8 ft), have in fact an average height (males) of 5 ft 10 in.'

It would be easy to say that Pigafetta and the Genoese pilot were exaggerating and leave it at that. But this would have been uncharacteristic of Pigafetta. I prefer to think of the exaggeration as something intrinsic to the occasion rather than as an effect supplied later for literary or personal vainglory. The magnification of the Tehuelche into a giant occurs right there and then, in the impact of that first meeting. The emptiness of the landscape, the lack of visual comparison, would also have been a factor.

Pigafetta really thought that he was dealing with a giant, really felt he was a waist-high pygmy beside him. That was how it seemed to him and to others. It was a kind of collective mirage conjured up out of the freezing deserts of Patagonia.

WE HAVE to imagine what it was like to deal with these experiences, thousands of miles away from all that was familiar. The sheer novelty of the New World—its people, its creatures, its flora—was challenging in a way we find hard to appreciate today, when so much is already prepared in our minds, already mapped out, the impact of difference softened to a pleasant notion of the picturesque.

How did the traveller deal with all this strangeness? He did so by finding some kind of precedent: an illusion, at least, of familiarity. And since there was often no actual precedent within his experience, he resorted to other sources—to the reservoir of travellers' tales, partly printed, partly oral; to the folk stories and legends of his European culture. Much of the 'discovery' of America involved the importing of images and ideas and indeed fantasies from Europe. Like the sea itself, *terra incognita* became a place of wonders, an 'invasion of unconscious contents'.

There are many instances of this in the writings of Columbus and Vespucci. Columbus's obsession with cannibals derives in part from his avid reading of early travel-writers such as Marco Polo and Sir John Mandeville, whose accounts abound in *anthropophagi*, or man-eaters. Columbus actually invented the word 'cannibal' himself—it was a mishearing of the tribal name 'Carib'—but it was inspired by an idea, a fear, he brought with him. He also reported the existence of a tribe of 'dog-faced men' inhabiting one of the Caribbean islands. These too are an echo of Marco Polo, who wrote of certain supposed inhabitants of the Andaman Islands: 'They have heads like dogs, and teeth and eyes like dogs; for I assure you that the whole aspect of their faces is that of big mastiffs.'

Another spectre conjured up by the New World was the Amazon. On his first voyage Columbus heard of certain female warriors inhabiting the island of Matinino (Martinique). As he understood it, they lived without men, they fought with bows and arrows, and they wore armour ('plates of copper'). He called them, naturally enough, 'Amazons' after the tribe of warrior women who in Greek mythology swept down from the hills of Scythia to occupy various Hellenic sites, notably the Isle of Lesbos. They shunned men, except once a year for the purposes of procreation; they killed male offspring; they cut off their right breasts to facilitate the pulling back of the bowstring (hence their name, from Greek *a mastos,* 'without breast'). These formidable women are to be found in all sorts of classical and medieval sources. They encode, not very opaquely, a whole range of male sexual fears and fantasies. Columbus himself gave a long and rather erotic gloss on the subject in his commentary on the *Historia Rerum* of Aeneas Sylvius. Later, on his first voyage, he imported them wholesale into the New World.

On his second voyage in 1496, Columbus actually encountered armed Carib women on the island of Guadeloupe. They were suitably fierce, but otherwise shared none of the characteristics of the classical Amazons. They did not live without men; they did not cut off their breasts. But by then the connection had been made, the legend was alive. It circulated, it gripped the imagination, and when, fifty years after Columbus, Francisco de Orellana encountered female warriors in the hinterlands of Peru, it was natural that he too should believe they were Amazons, and equally natural, in this nameless continent, that the river he was travelling down should thereafter be called the Amazon.

The cannibal, the dog-faced man, the Amazon dominatrix: these are some of the chimera that haunted the traveller in the New World. (The cannibal is not quite a chimera, of course, but the practice of cannibalism was certainly not rife in the Caribbean.) The reader of Amerigo Vespucci's *Lettera delle Isole Novamente Trovate,* meanwhile, would learn that there were also dragons in the New World. Vespucci had seen one being captured and cooked by Brazilian Indians:

Their feet are long and thick, and armed with big claws; they have a hard skin and are of various colours; they have the muzzle and aspect of a serpent, and from their snouts there rises a crest like a saw which runs along the middle of the back as far as the tip of the tail.

This dragon, whose 'appearance was so foul that we marvelled at its loathsomeness', was in reality an iguana.

There is a common thread to these New World prodigies. They seem to represent an unconscious fear of being devoured, swallowed up, a fear of disappearing into the mysterious otherness of the New World. The traditional giants of legend and fairy tale also have this devouring aspect: 'I'll grind his bones to make my bread.'

LIKE THOSE earlier travellers, Antonio Pigafetta set off on his journey into the unknown with certain preconceptions about what he would find there. He knew of the 'great and awful things of the ocean'. We cannot be certain what he had read— the only text he actually mentions in his narrative is Aristotle's *De Coelo et Mundo*—but it is a reasonable assumption that he knew the writings of Amerigo Vespucci, the Florentine explorer who is commemorated in the name 'America' (largely on the basis of his spurious claim to have landed on the American mainland in 1497, a year before Columbus's arrival).

Vespucci was, like Pigafetta, a man of some cultivation and social standing—his sister Simonetta was the swan-necked beauty who was the model for Botticelli's *Birth of Venus* and

for various other Renaissance painters including Piero di Cos-
imo. And his influential *Lettera delle Isole Novamente Trovate,*
published in Florence in about 1505, could easily have been
the source of Pigafetta's giants (in the sense that Polo was the
source of Columbus's cannibals). Among its descriptions is an
encounter with 'giants' on the island of Curaçao. Vespucci and
his companions first saw five women 'so lofty in stature that
we gazed at them in astonishment'. They were 'taller than a
tall man'. The travellers were tempted to capture them, 'to
carry them to Castille as a prodigy', but were scared off by the
emergence of a group of men who were even bigger. These
men 'went entirely naked'. They were 'so well-built that it was
a famous sight to see them, but they put us into such uneasiness
that we would much rather have been back in our ships'.

Vespucci concludes: 'I call that island the Isle of Giants, because of their great size.' The legend 'Gigantes' was duly appended to Curaçao in various early sixteenth-century maps. It
is not hard to see Pigafetta's experiences in Patagonia as an
echo, a confirmation of what he had read in Vespucci's *Lettera.*
He had anticipated the presence of giants in the New World,
and suddenly, with a lurch of fear in his stomach, he saw one.

There is another book to be considered, one that may hold
a key to the name of the region, Patagonia. According to Pigafetta it was Magellan himself who coined this name ('The
Captain named this kind of people Pataghom'). The customary
interpretation of this is that *patagon* means 'big foot' (from
Spanish *pata,* a foot or paw), and that it relates to the footwear

of the natives: huge galoshes of guanaco hide packed with straw. An Argentinian scholar, Professor Gonzáles Diaz of Buenos Aires, suggests another derivation, which is that the 'giants' of the region reminded Magellan (or perhaps Pigafetta) of a creature that featured in a popular romance, *Primaleon of Greece*. In this, the hero Primaleon sails to a faraway island where the natives eat raw flesh and wear animal skins. They live in fear of a huge half-human monster 'with a head like a dog' in the interior of the island. Primaleon heroically vanquishes it, and carries it back to his homeland, 'Polonia', where it is civilized by the kind attentions of good Princess Zephira.

A Spanish edition of *Primaleon* was published in 1512, seven years before Magellan's departure. Its imagery has a strong tinge of the New World about it. The monster with the bestial features is called the Great Patagon. Is this the source of Magellan's name for the giants of San Julián? Is this another of those precedents the early traveller reached for when faced with the extraordinary?

THERE WAS a period of nearly three months between the first sighting of the Tehuelche giant and the fleet's departure from San Julián. During this time Pigafetta came to know two of the giants quite well. They were baptized and given Christian names—Juan and Pablo—and were kept on board ship. In Pigafetta's text they continue to seem like fairy-tale giants: 'they ate a large basketful of biscuit, and rats without skinning them, and they drank half a bucket of water at one go', but they also begin to emerge as human characters. Of Juan, Pigafetta writes:

> He was a gracious and amiable person, who liked to dance and leap. When he leaped he made holes in the ground where he landed to the depth of a palm. He was a long time with us. This giant pronounced the name of Jesus, the Paternoster, the Ave Maria, and his own name as clearly as we did. But he had a terribly strong and loud voice.

Over the weeks and months of the bitter Patagonian winter Pigafetta observed them, conversed with them, and learned something of Tehuelche society and culture:

> They have no houses, but have huts made of the skins of the animals with which they clothe themselves, and they go hither and thither with these huts of theirs as the Egyptians [i.e. gypsies] do.
>
> When they go hunting they wear a cord of cotton around their heads from which they hang their arrows, and they tie up their members inside their bodies on account of the severe cold. They eat a certain white powder made of roots [probably a form of manioc]. Sometimes they eat thistles.
>
> When these giants have a stomach ache they do not take medicine, but put an arrow, about two foot long, down their throats, and then they vomit up a green bile mixed with blood. When they have a headache they make a cut across the forehead and also on the arms and legs, to draw blood from several parts of their bodies. One of the two who were in our ship

told me that the blood did not choose to remain in the place of the body where the pain was felt.

Of their pagan religion he writes:

> He [Pablo] told us, by signs, that he had seen devils with two horns on their heads, and long hair down to their feet, who breathed fire out of their mouths and their rumps. The greatest of these devils is called in their language Setebos.

This in turn explains an earlier sentence about the giants: 'They began to be enraged, and to foam like bulls, crying out very loud, Setebos.' This sentence was translated by the Elizabethan travel writer Richard Eden, who included an abbreviated English version of Pigafetta in his compilation, *The History of Travaile,* published in 1577. This in turn was read by Shakespeare, and used for his own version of the New World native, Caliban in *The Tempest:* '0 Setebos! These be brave spirits indeed.'

Thus Caliban, anagrammatically a cannibal, is also in some measure a Patagonian; and thus the reality of this encounter on the shores of Argentina merges back into the fictional world from which it partly arose.

Towards the end of Pigafetta's stay in San Julián there comes a moment of great poignancy, a reaching out across the huge cultural differences between Europe and the New World, across the curiously blurred frontier between the real and the fictional. The giant called Pablo fell sick. He was in a cabin of the ship. Pigafetta was there with him:

> He asked me for capac, or bread, for this is the name they give to that root which they use for bread; and for olla, or water.

And when he saw me write these names down, and afterwards ask him for other names, he understood what I was doing with the pen in my hand.

At this point, the relationship between them seems at last to become whole. The point of view changes. Suddenly we see Pigafetta through the giant's eyes: a small, dark-eyed, rather earnest man with this curiously plumed implement poised above the paper.

This moment of illumination enabled Pigafetta to produce a brief but impressive dictionary entitled, in the French manuscript, *Vocables des Géants Pathagoniens*. This is a list of ninety-one words and phrases in 'Patagonian'—a lexicon quite unprecedented in the European literature on the New World at this date. About half of the words translated are parts of the body, always easy to establish on a rudimentary point-and-tell basis. After anatomy is exhausted the list moves on: to fire, smoke, ice, wind and stars; to fish, dog, wolf, goose (i.e. penguin) and oyster. Pigafetta notes the guttural tone of the language—the words are 'pronounced in the throat'—but perhaps the keynote of this lexicon is not the strangeness of the sounds but the communality of the world they describe: a sense of what is shared by these two men.

Pigafetta concludes: 'All these words were given to me by this giant,' and one is touched by his brusque acknowledgement of a debt, of a gift he has received from this monster who turned out, after all, to be a man not much different from himself.

★   ★   ★

THERE FOLLOW the maritime adventures which have earned this voyage its place in history—the discovery of the southern passage into the Pacific now called the Straits of Magellan; the long months of privation as they drifted on westwards towards the Spice Islands; the death of Magellan in a skirmish with natives in the Philippines; and, on 6 September 1522, the final return to Seville of a single ship, the *Victoria,* and just eighteen of the 240 men who had set out three years earlier.

Among the survivors was the resourceful reporter Antonio Pigafetta. At Valladolid he presented to the Spanish King 'neither gold nor silver, but things much more precious in the eyes of so great a sovereign'. Chief among these was 'a book written by my hand of all the things that had occurred day by day on our voyage'. This original journal does not seem to have survived. The manuscripts that do survive—three in French and one in Italian—are essentially a paraphrase of it: 'I have reduced into this small book the principal things, as well as I could.'

In 1523 he was fêted at a grand reception in Venice. He was also admitted into the Order of the Knights of Rhodes, and signed himself thereafter with a flourish: Antonio Pigafetta *Cavaliere.* The following year he received permission from the Venetian Senate to publish his account of the voyage, but he does not seem to have done so. He retired back to Vicenza, the town of his birth. The aftermath of his great adventure is obscure; one perhaps discerns a note of exhaustion.

On the front wall of his house, on the street that was then

called Via dalla Luna and which is now called Via Pigafetta, he had a plaque put up. It is still there, beside the graceful Romanesque doorway, though the house itself is now the premises of a smart dress-shop. One might expect it to say something grand and triumphal about circumnavigation, about the great and awful things of the ocean, about going to the uttermost ends of the earth and back again.

But all he chooses to say, in somewhat ungrammatical French, is: '*Il n'est rose sans épines.*' There is no rose without thorns. If there is some deeper resonance in this, it escapes me. Perhaps the resonance lies precisely in its simplicity: he had travelled so far to discover this small truth.

He died in Vicenza in 1535, not yet 50 years old.

tudor image-makers

/ **IF WE** will have anything
well painted, carved or em-
broidered,' grumbled Sir Thomas Elyot in 1531, 'we abandon
our own countrymen and resort unto strangers.' His complaint
is borne out by *Dynasties*, the Tate Gallery's fascinating exhibition of painting in Tudor and Jacobean England. The home-
grown talent is here—Nicholas Hilliard, George Gower, Inigo
Jones, William Larkin, Sir Nathaniel Bacon, etc—but the exhibition is dominated, statistically at least, by foreign artists,
mainly Dutch and Flemish.

Some of these 'strangers' were visitors, like Holbein and Van
Dyck, but many settled here and became naturalised English-
men or 'denizens'. They brought an invigorating new

Independent, 1995

range of techniques that transformed English art. Most of the paintings and drawings on show here are portraits, but the exhibition is not the dour gallery of Tudor mug-shots that this might suggest. They come in a marvellous variety of styles, and in all shapes and sizes, from the fastidious miniatures of Hilliard and Isaac Oliver, painted on two-inch snippets of vellum glued onto bits of playing-card, to the tall, lush, overbearing canvases of Stuart court artists.

There is also a variety of ideas as to what a portrait is, and what it should say about its subject. We see here, as Karen Hearn says in her catalogue, 'an ebb and flow in the desire for naturalistic representation'. Among the earliest works are exquisite Holbein sketches from the 1530s, where every hair on a young woman's eyebrows seems alive, but for much of the Tudor period the capturing of physical and personal detail seems almost incidental. The portrait is seen more as a mode of display, a finely tuned statement of the sitter's status and allegiance, a creating of his or her 'image' in the public relations sense of the word we use today.

These are pictures to be read as much as viewed, their messages signalled in costume details, Latin mottoes and heraldic devices, and in a range of symbolic props in which everything from gillyflowers to goldfinches has an emblematic meaning.

The chief 'dynasties' portrayed here are the Tudors and Stuarts, but there is a powerful presence of those other great English families—aristocrats, *arrivistes,* merchants, politicians— whose flair, energy and greed were as decisive in the history of the period as the policies of the monarchs themselves.

One of the most arresting pictures is the Cobham family portrait. Painted in 1567 by an unnamed artist in the service of the Countess of Warwick, it shows William Brooke, 10th Lord Cobham, at the age of about 40, together with his wife and sister, his six young children, and their assorted pets. It is mealtime, specifically dessert: a scene of domestic togetherness, but painted with that deliberate waxy stiffness, that sense of ceremonial hush, which takes one away from the everyday and into the realm of the painting's messages and meanings.

The message is precisely dynastic. The Latin inscription compares Lord Cobham to Old Testament patriarchs like Jacob and Job. 'God grant that the line of Cobham beget many off-spring such as Joseph.' The prayer is already answered by the clutch of doll-like children below; indeed the whole composition has the diagrammatic look of a family tree.

On the table there are fruit—apples, pears, grapes, walnuts: a tribute to the prolific orchards of Cohham Hall, and a re-statement of the picture's message of fruitfulness and dynastic harvest. Another symbolic prop is the diamond pendant Lady Cobham wears, in the shape of an ocean-going ship. This sug-gests another kind of harvest: the riches of maritime trade filling the Cobham coffers. The parrot and the monkey—imported New World pets—are part of the same idea. The ship also has an emblematic meaning of happiness, alluding to a Roman emblem showing a ship named *Felicitas*.

The Cobham portrait seems almost a kind of talisman, an invoking of familial health, wealth and stability in an age of slippery fortunes. In fact, there are historical ironies to the picture. The title was inherited by Henry, seen here as a two-year-old with a puppy on his lap. Implicated in a conspiracy against King James in 1603, he was attainted for treason and stripped of his peerage, thus bringing to an abrupt end the dynastic aspirations expressed in this painting. We catch the Cobhams in a moment of eminence which proves somewhat temporary. Portraits of the Catholic Howards have a similar resonance, particularly the canvas of the Earl of Surrey, the nobleman-poet, bursting with confidence and Italianate elegance. It was painted in 1546, when he was 29; a year later he was beheaded on a trumped up charge of treason.

The Brookes and the Howards were powerful but expendable satellites around the central dynasty of the monarchy. Royal portraits form the heart of the exhibition. The earliest (c 1500) is the poignant little portrait of Prince Arthur, Henry VIII's elder brother, who died at the age of 15. This was rediscovered a couple of years ago, at Castle Forbes in Ireland, and is seen here for the first time.

An entire room is devoted to images of Queen Elizabeth. She was the most cultish of all the Tudors, and fully exploited the propagandist element of portraiture. Most of the surviving pictures of her are known by some symbolic device or allusion. Here we have the 'Armada portrait', and the rather ghostly 'Sieve portrait'. The most striking is the 'Phoenix portrait' (c 1576) attributed to Hilliard, though it is not the symbolic paraphernalia that catches the eye—the phoenix jewel and the Tudor rose—but the brilliant detail of Hilliard's workmanship. The gold embroidery of the dress is represented by paint, principally lead-tin yellow, rather than by the actual gold leaf used a generation earlier (for example, in the 1544 portrait of Mary Tudor). This kind of technical advance contributed to the growing autonomy of the artist, enabling him to represent precious materials without having to afford them.

The portraits of Elizabeth do not invite personal or biographical interpretations, but the study of King James, by the Dutchman Adrian Vanson, certainly does. Painted in 1595, it shows a very human James at the age of 29 (though some of its unusual intimacy is a result of a later cutting-down of the picture). The face is sallow, the gaze weary, the mouth thin and ironic. One thinks of the personal traumas of his childhood: the murders, the night flights, the execution of his mother. He seems slightly slumped. His tall sugar-loaf hat is tipped back, giving him the air of a melancholy young *boulevardier* resting between bouts of absinthe.

Right beside this is a portrait of the wily Sir Robert Cecil, painted by Johan De Critz in about 1602, on the eve of James's succession to the English throne, which Cecil as Secretary of State had done so much to engineer. Here is a man in control of his own destiny—far more so, one feels, than the droopy young king next door. On his table are folded dispatches, a seal-bag, a bell to summon his amanuenses and clerks. This is the new man, the bureaucrat, the political string-puller.

In the portraits of Cobham and Cecil, and in the lesser-known merchants and gentry staring huffily out, one gets a sombre, mafioso sense of Elizabethan power-mongering. But there is plenty of the more flamboyant side, the peacockery and swagger, as in Hilliard's famous miniature of George Clifford, 3rd Earl of Cumberland, in an extravagant costume of azure and gold embroidered with astrological and alchemical devices. He is dressed up for the Accession Day Tilt, a mockchivalric festival in which aspiring courtiers jousted for the Queen's favours.

Cumberland—an inveterate gambler and a courageous seacaptain—epitomises the panache of the era. Even more eyecatching is Richard Sackville, 3rd Earl of Dorset, painted by William Larkin in 'cloth of silver embroidered all over in slips of satin, black and gold'. He is the perfect dandy, from his doily-like ruff down to his pom-pommed pantofles. This probably shows him at the wedding of Princess Elizabeth and the Elector Palatine, on 14 February 1613, at which it was said he 'dazzled the eyes of all who saw'.

Among all the monarchs and magnates are a few pictures of the artists themselves. Easily missed is the wry self-portrait by George Gower (1579). It is the only large-size self-portrait in existence by a 16th-century British artist. He holds a palette and a paintbrush. An inscription celebrates his work 'by pencil's trade' and the rewards it has brought him: 'What parents bore by just renown, my skill maintains.'

And so a new professional group edges up the increasingly crowded and competitive social ladder. Essentially of artisan class—servers of apprenticeship, members of guilds, guarders of trade secrets—they have acquired an indispensable role as the image-makers of Tudor high society.

marlowe's boyhood

T**HE LATE** William Urry knew more about Christopher Marlowe's early life in Canterbury than anyone. His 'forthcoming book' on the subject was mentioned by one of Marlowe's biographers as long ago as 1965. Here at last it is, seven years after his death, edited from drafts by his former colleague Andrew Butcher. The text runs to less than a hundred pages, but there are many appendices and source-notes, and anyway these hundred pages of dense documentary detail are worth a thousand of theorising.

Our historical knowledge of Elizabethan writers like Marlowe ultimately rests on this kind of deep archival work. Toiling through mouldy reams of municipal Latin, poring over act

London Review of Books, 1988

books and close rolls, pleas and recognizances, baptisms and burials, borough-mote surveys and consistorial court proceedings, scholars like Urry provide a constant supply of rich contextual trivia, and just occasionally, down some documentary back-way, they stumble upon the great and famous, and retrieve some precious nugget of raw information about them. The classic instance in Marlowe's case was the unearthing by Leslie Hotson, in 1925, of the coroner's inquest on Marlowe's death. While Urry has made no comparable discovery—perhaps no one will—he has lit up many small corners of Marlowe's life, particularly of his childhood.

Christopher Marlowe—or Marley, in the more common contemporary spelling, the one he used in his only extant signature—was born in the parish of St George's, Canterbury, in February 1564. He was the son of John Marlowe, shoemaker, and Katherine *née* Arthur, a Dover woman. They had nine children, though only five survived childhood. Christopher was the eldest son, and after the death of his sister Mary in 1568, the eldest child in the family. His father was 'rowdy, quarrelsome, awkward, improvident, busy, self-assertive and too clever by half', in Urry's estimate. He appears often in local records, sometimes in positions of minor responsibility—warden of the Shoemakers' Company, sidesman at the parish church, constable at Westgate—but more often when being sued for debt, nonpayment of rent, or breach of the peace. He was fined for giving his apprentice Lactantius Preston a bloody nose in 1576, and was himself assaulted by another apprentice a few years later. It is hard to avoid seeing Marlowe's touchy aggressive temper—intellectual and physical—prefigured in his father. His sister Anne seems to have been a handful as well. Like him she was known as a 'swearer' and 'blasphemer of the name of God', and in 1626, well into her fifties, she set about an unfortunate neighbour, one Prowde, with a staff and a dagger.

Marlowe's origins were provincial and artisan: an earlier generation in Canterbury were tanners; Christopher's sisters married a tailor, a shoemaker and a glover. This tough, industrious class nurtured much of the budding literary talent of the time: the Elizabethan leather industry provided a livelihood, not only for Marlowe's family, but also for that of Robert Greene and William Shakespeare, sons respectively of a Norwich saddler and a Stratford glover. Even here in Canterbury there were other young writers growing up: John Lyly, son of Peter Lyly, clerk to the consistorial court; and Stephen Gosson, a joiner's son. We have here a miniature blueprint for late Elizabethan theatrical tastes: Marlowe the tragedian, whose thunderous poetry packed them in at the public theatres; Lyly the author of dapper courtly comedies for the boy-actors of St Paul's; and Gosson the controversialist, whose *Schoole of Abuse* (1579) was a violent attack on the theatre, and provided a prototype for the Puritan attitudes that were to dog Marlowe's brief career.

In terms of Marlowe biography, Dr Urry's canvas is less partial than might appear. Marlowe was getting on for seventeen when he left Canterbury for Cambridge University in late 1580. He died at the age of 29, so this study covers a good half of his life—often the more obscure half in a distant historical figure. Urry recovers the young Marlowe's immediate human and social surroundings: extended family, neighbours, apprentices, schoolfellows. He reels off the names of the Marlowes' neighbours as if he were doffing his cap to them in the street: Alderman Rose the woollen-draper; Harmon Verson the immigrant glazier; Laurence Applegate the tailor, who spoke 'bawdy words' about Mistress Hurt; Goodman Shaw the basketmaker, into whose house John Marlowe stormed one evening in 1579 and said, 'Michael Shaw thou art a thief, and so I will prove thee to be'; and Gregory Roose the capper, husband to the local midwife Goodwife Roose, who probably brought Christopher Marlowe into the world.

Though compact—population about 3500—Elizabethan Canterbury was a cosmopolitan city. Its ecclesiastical eminence drew visitors from all over Europe, and its position on the through-road from Dover to London brought a broader cross-section of travellers, soldiers, sailors and sturdy vagabonds. Like many cities, it hosted Protestant war-refugees from France and the Low Countries. A wave of French Huguenots arrived after the St Bartholomew's Day Massacre in 1572, an event Marlowe later worked over in his lurid political drama, *The Massacre at Paris*.

Religion loomed large in Canterbury. The only book in the family home—at least by the time of John Marlowe's death in 1605—was the Bible. In St George's parish, lying between the cathedral and the city's eastern gate, Marlowe grew up literally in the shadow of the Church. He witnessed its finest pomps, also no doubt its grisly punishments. He became one of its most reckless critics, scoffing at the 'bugbeares and hobgoblins' of superstition, and dangerously arguing that religion was just a political tool 'to keep men in awe'. Here too, Urry gives a local, human face to religious controversy. At King's School, which Marlowe entered on a £4-a-year scholarship in 1578, his fellow pupils included Samuel Kennett, who became a Catholic exile and missionary, and died a Benedictine monk in 1612; and Henry Jacob, who later founded one of the first Congregationalist Churches in England. Nearby lived a young Puritan called Robert Cushman, a grocer's assistant. Many years later he returned from exile in Holland and was the prime mover in the hiring of the ship *Mayflower.*

Marlowe's first headmaster at King's was a Cambridge man, John Gresshop, and an interesting document published here is the catalogue of Gresshop's library, drawn up on his death in 1580. It contained over three hundred and fifty volumes— nothing like the Mortlake library of Dr John Dee (four thousand volumes) or the thousand-plus books collected by Lords Burghley and Lumley, but it shows the kind of reading available to a bright young scholar. There are the plays of Plautus and Terence, the poems of Juvenal and Ovid, a strong Italian presence including Boccaccio, Petrarch, Valla and Ficino. There is More's *Utopia,* Munster's *Cosmographia,* and the works of Chaucer. One senses the emancipation, the new mental world opening up for the cobbler's son. Among the theological tracts on Gresshop's shelves was John Proctor's *Fal of the Late Arrian,* a confutation of Arian views which questioned the divinity of Christ. This was already an old book, published in 1549, but it contained large chunks of the heresy it was written to confute. An Arian manuscript, drawn verbatim from this book, was among the papers seized at Thomas Kyd's lodgings on 11 May 1593. These 'vile hereticall conceipts', as the investigators called them, were said by Kyd to be Marlowe's. They had got 'shuffled' with Kyd's papers when the two writers were sharing a chamber in 1591. A week later Marlowe was himself summoned before the Privy Council for questioning. Those 'hereticall conceipts' were certainly part of the matter: in the murky political context of 1593 such ideas had acquired new dangerousness, especially in association with Marlowe. Before the end of the month, he lay dead in Deptford.

After his departure for Cambridge, just two further visits to Canterbury remain on record. On a Sunday morning in November 1585 he was at the house of Katherine Benchkin on Stour Street, together with his father, his brother-in-law John Moore, and his uncle Thomas Arthur. There, in the parlour, Mistress Benchkin asked him to read out her new will, which he did 'plainely and distinktly', and shortly afterwards signed the will in witness. The will was discovered by another Canterbury burrower, Frank Tyler, in 1939. It is the only known example of Marlowe's signature, and provides, in turn, calligraphic proof that the 'Collier Leaf'—a manuscript fragment of *The Massacre at Paris,* now in the Folger Library—is in Marlowe's own hand.

Marlowe's last recorded spell in Canterbury was in September 1592. Typically, it was a fight that makes it memorable.

On Friday, 15 September, close to the corner of Mercery Lane, Marlowe attacked William Corkine, tailor, with a staff and a dagger. Marlowe's father, ironically, was acting as local constable at that time: possibly he had to arrest his son, certainly he paid the 12*d* surety required to keep Christopher out of jail. Corkine sued for assault, but by the time it came to court they had patched up their differences, and the case was dismissed. Twenty years later, a William Corkine published a lute accompaniment to Marlowe's famous lyric, 'Come Live With Me'. This was probably the Canterbury tailor's son.

Marlowe had only one brother, Thomas. He was four when Marlowe left for Cambridge, 16 at the time of the Corkine fracas. To him Marlowe must have been half a stranger, someone who returned home from time to time, trailing notoriety from London. Thomas may have died young too—there is no mention of him in his mother's will, 1605—but he may just be the Thomas Marloe who travelled to America in the ship *Jonathan,* and who was living in 1624 at a settlement near Jamestown, Virginia, breathing the freer air of America that would so much have suited brother Kit.

Urry's coverage of Marlowe's later career is sketchier, but one body of interesting new material concerns Eleanor Bull, in whose house at Deptford Strand Marlowe was killed. The evidence increasingly suggests she was a lady of some substance. She was the widow of a minor official at nearby Deptford Manor, cousin of one of the Queen's gentlewomen, Blanche Parry, and perhaps distantly related to Lord Burghley himself. As Urry says, this finally dissipates the romance image of Mistress Bull as a 'poor ale-house keeper eking out a squalid existence at Deptford docks'. So far this line of enquiry proves nothing directly about the circumstances of the killing, but it tends to shift the tone of the incident yet further away from the conventional—and official—version, which blamed his death on a drunken brawl over the 'reckoning'.

Marlowe was an extraordinary man, yet his life, like everyone else's, constantly intersected with ordinariness. This book tells us about him because it tells us what it was like to live in that decade, in that street, in that income-bracket. In his perceptive introduction Andrew Butcher suggests that this kind of close-focus contextual study is now really the front line in Elizabethan literary history. It recovers the contingencies—the 'formative tensions', as he puts it—of a writer's life. It finds him not in quill-wielding solitude, but precisely at his points of contact, his mingling with certain very particular sectors and groupings of Elizabethan life, shaping them and being shaped by them, each point of contact leaving its forensic traces. Some may find Dr Urry's book too dense with detail. But the detail is a kind of intimacy, and in the end he gives us a portrait more human, more actual, than the psychologising and bio-crit of more conventional biography.

tamquam explorator

BEN JONSON is remem-bered as a master of English comedy, but you would hardly think so from his portrait. The earliest dateable likeness is the engraving by Robert Vaughan, done in the mid 1620s, when Jonson was around 50. The face is jowly, bearded, dour, heavily lived-in. The shadowed eyes remind me of photos of Tony Hancock. Comedy, they seem to say, is no laughing matter. It was one of Jonson's sayings that 'he would not flatter, though he saw death', and his look seems to challenge the artist not to flatter him either. You can see the glisten on his skin from too much canary wine, and the warts and blemishes which more malicious caricaturists like Thomas Dekker dwell on: 'a face full of pockey-holes and

London Review of Books, 1989

pimples . . . a most ungodly face, like a rotten russet apple when 'tis bruised'. You can confirm that, as Aubrey noted, he had one eye bigger and lower than the other. And you can guess at what was by then his vast bulk. In his youth he was tall and rangy, a 'hollow-cheekt scrag', but by middle age he had swelled to a corpulent 19 stone. In his poem 'My Picture Left in Scotland' (1619) he mocks his unwieldy frame—

> *So much waist as she cannot embrace*
> *My mountaine belly and my rockye face*

—yet seems also to celebrate its craggy solidity. This sense of solidity and stature is also conveyed in the portrait. Here, in every sense, is a big man.

Even his literary greatness seems sometimes more a bigness, a triumph of volume and stamina. His career spanned three reigns and four decades, from the first flexing of comic power in *The Isle of Dogs* (1597) to the last melancholy fragments of *The Sad Shepherd,* probably written in the final year of his life. During that time he wrote 18 plays, 37 masques and court entertainments, two volumes of poetry and a volume of epigrams. This list does not include the lost plays from his days as one of Henslowe's hacks at the Rose, nor the mass of work unpublished at his death: over a hundred miscellaneous pieces of verse, a translation of Horace's *Ars Poetica,* an English grammar, and the compendium of jottings, musings and mini-essays later collected under the title of *Timber* (or 'Discoveries Made Upon Men and Matter').

In an age when most writers burned out young, Jonson kept on going. Right at the end, embattled by debt and alcoholism, half-paralysed by a stroke, he was still at work. Among his last pieces was the *English Grammar,* published posthumously in 1640. It shows him still niggling away at the nuts and bolts of the language, purifying that 'sterling English diction' which Coleridge praised in him, involving himself in such orthographic minutiae as the superiority of the 'serviceable *k*' over 'this halting Q, with her waiting-woman *u* after her'. Also among his papers were fragments of two plays: the pastorale called *The Sad Shepherd,* and a chronicle-play, *Mortimer His Fall.* The printed text of the latter concludes curtly, 'He dy'd, and left it unfinished,' furnishing an apocryphal vision of the aged maestro finally keeling over with the ink still wet on his quill. It was not probably like that, but Jonson encourages these vignettes.

He died in August 1637, aged 65, at the gate-house in Westminster where he lived his last years with a pet fox and a drunken housekeeper. His funeral was attended by 'the greatest part of the nobilitie and gentry', and a volume of memorial odes, *Jonsonus Virbius,* was published the following year. Here his disciples—the 'Tribe of Ben', as they were called—praise him as the 'great Instructor', the 'voice most echoed by consenting men'. A generation later, in his essay 'Of Dramatick Poesy', Dryden singled him out as the 'greatest man of the last age'.

These are literary judgments. Posterity has preferred a briefer, more elusive epitaph. As his grave at Westminster Abbey was being covered, a passer-by, Sir Jack Young, noticed that the headstone was still blank. He 'gave the fellow eighteen pence' to cut an inscription. It read simply: 'O Rare Benn Jonson'.

LIKE THE portraitist, Jonson's biographer has to achieve a kind of dual image. He has to convey Jonson's huge stature, his pre-eminence as a public literary figure, yet also to reveal something of the private flaws and tensions that lay behind it. It is odd how few have risen to this challenge. C. H. Herford's memoir in the 11-volume Oxford *Ben Jonson,* published in 1925, has remained the best account long after modern scholarship has found omissions and errors in it. Chute's biography (1953) is too heavy on the rumbust, and Rosalind Miles's (1986) is an accumulation of scholarly detail that is never quite a 'life'. Now at last we have a biography that pulls out all the right stops. David Riggs provides a fastidious, challenging and compassionate reading of the man. Not everyone will agree with some of its psychiatrist's couch diagnoses—anal fixations, step-father traumas, and so on—though personally I find them convincing.

There is something daunting about Jonson, something that rejects you. This, too, you feel in his portrait. You even feel it in his comedies: their core of harshness, the derision and punishment that go with the laughter. Also the sense of huge verbal labour in them, which is always contrasted with Shakespeare's agility and flow. This note is already sounded by Dryden, who styles Jonson the Virgil of English drama to Shakespeare's Homer, and adds tellingly: 'I admire him, but I love Shakespeare.' This perhaps articulates the basic problem. You cannot quite love Ben Jonson. In fact, sometimes you're not even sure if you like him.

There were plenty who didn't at the time. There is a rich store of contemporary material on him, and much of it is disparaging. The earliest and funniest is the caricature of Jonson as 'Horace' in Thomas Dekker's comedy *Satiromastix*. This played in 1601, when Jonson was 29. Subtitled 'The Untrussing of the Humorous Poet' (referring to Jonson's popular 'comedy of humours'), it gives a scurrilous portrait of Jonson in the first swagger of literary success. Dekker dwells on his ugliness— a face 'like the cover of a warming pan', a voice that 'sounds so i'th'nose'—and portrays him as a seedy penny-a-liner whose only aim is to 'skrue and wriggle himself into great men's familiarity'. Dekker's purpose is to give this 'thornie-tooth'd satyricall rascal' a dose of his own medicine, but somehow he ends up seconding the vigour and charisma of his target, as when he bids Horace not to 'dippe your manners in too much sawce, nor at table to fling epigrams, emblemes or play-speeches about you lyke hayle-stones'.

This was one of the exchanges in the so-called 'War of the Theatres'. Shakespeare was briefly involved in this, and according to one well-informed contemporary, he gave that 'pestilent fellow' Jonson a 'purge which made him bewray his credit'. Historians have wondered what form this literary laxative took. Some suggest that Jonson is guyed as big morose

Ajax in *Troilus and Cressida* (with, according to Ernst Honig-mann, the diminutive epigrammist John Weever as Thersites). Others say Jonson is a model for Jaques, the embittered satirist of Arden ('They that are most galled with my folly, they most must laugh'). Riggs offers, rather unconvincingly, Malvolio in *Twelfth Night*.

The richest contemporary account of Jonson is the record of his conversations with the Scottish poet, William Drum-mond. In the summer of 1618, Jonson walked from London to Scotland (Francis Bacon remarking drily that 'he loved not to see poesy go on other feet than poetical *dactyllus* and *spon-daeus*'). Having been fêted in Edinburgh, he passed a few pleasant weeks in the autumn as Drummond's guest at Haw-thornden. There he bent the Scotsman's ear with a barrage of anecdotes, aphorisms, jokes and libels. Drummond duly tran-scribed, preserving the authentic timbre of Jonson's table-talk, highly seasoned and doubtless well-pickled (drink, Drummond tartly observed, 'is one of the elements in which he liveth'). The *Conversations* offers a crabby review of the current literary scene—Donne 'deserved hanging' for his metrical liberties, Shakespeare 'wanted art', Sharpham, Day and Dekker were 'all rogues', Samuel Daniel was 'a good honest man, but no poet'—but more importantly it provides the rudiments of autobiography. In Drummond, as in every-one else, there is that uncertain reaction. He is awe-struck yet curiously disappointed. Jonson's flamboyance is there— 'passionately kynde and angry, careless either to gane or keep'—but Drummond finds him a 'bragger' and a 'scorner'.

He is 'oppressed with fantasie'. He would rather 'lose a friend than a jest'.

THE ACHIEVEMENT of Jonson's greatest comedies—*Volpone* (1606), *The Alchemist* (1610), *Bartholomew Fair* (1613) and *The Devil is an Ass* (1616)—is their openness to social realities. He harnessed the texture and parlance of Elizabethan street-life, and fashioned a rich yet austere poetry out of

> *Deedes and language such as men doe use,*
> *And persons such as Comoedie would chuse*
> *When she would shew an image of the times.*

This pungency was to him a dramatic requisite every bit as important as the Classical notions of structural 'unity' he insisted on. As he put it in the introduction to *Bartholomew Fair*, you cannot write about a day at the fair 'without a language that savours of Smithfield, the booth and the pig-broath'. Jonson's achievement is about what literature can use, what it can include. One of the lessons of his life, Riggs says, 'is that everything is of use.'

His early life, as stormy as the rest of it, seems in some ways the perfect apprenticeship for this. By the time he turned to playwriting in the mid-1590s, Jonson had seen something of the seamier side of Elizabethan life. He had grown up on Hartshorn Lane, a street-cum-sewer running between Strand and the Thames. He had worked as a bricklayer, apprenticed to his stepfather, Robert Brett. He had fought with the English troops in the Low Countries, later boasting that he had killed an enemy 'in the face of both camps', and 'taken *opima spolia* from him'. He had married, and held a new-born daughter in his arms, and buried her six months later:

> *This grave partakes the fleshly birth,*
> *Which cover lightly, gentle earth.*

His actual literary apprenticeship (like Shakespeare's, probably) took the form of acting in the provinces. Dekker liked to remind him of his lowly beginnings, when 'thou amblest in leather pilch by a play-wagon in the highway, and tookst mad Jeronimoes part to get service amongst the mimickes.' He must have been good: Hieronimo in Kyd's evergreen *Spanish Tragedy* was a plum part. His first mention in the accounts of Philip Henslowe, manager of the Rose theatre, is the loan of £4 in 'redey mony' to 'Bengemen Iohnson, player'.

I wish he was here to pass comment on latest developments at the Rose. He would hardly be surprised: this smothering of the theatre in an office-block seems a perfect Jonsonian device. His view of Jacobean social values was bleak. He sees a scrabbling, acquisitive society, a society of victims and predators. Its predominant 'humours' are greed and delusion, personified onstage by a comic cast of scavengers and speculators, legacy-hunters and gold-diggers, Meercrafts and Eithersides, Sir Moth Interests and Sir Politic Would-bes. The issues today at the

Rose are Jonson's issues: Thatcherite humours, political double-speak, and the things they destroy.

Riggs reminds us of the courage that went into his theatrical 'image of the times'. Chaotic though it was, Jonson's career has a cumulative pattern: one of questioning and defining the poet's public role, testing the scope of his comment. This was edge-work with very real dangers attached to it. His first known work was *The Isle of Dogs,* co-written with Thomas Nashe, performed in July 1597. The play is lost. Its nascent comic skills cannot be judged, but its political bite is clear enough. The play was immediately suppressed by the Privy Council as 'lewd, seditious and sclandrous'. All the playhouses in the London area were shut down, and Jonson and two of the actors spent ten weeks in jail in the Marshalsea. He later boasted of his obstinate silence: his 'judges'—who included rackmaster Richard Topcliffe—'could get nothing of him to all their demands but Aye and No'. He was also plagued by prison informers, 'two damn'd villains' who tried to wheedle seditious sentiments out of him. One of these was Robert Poley, the government agent who was present at the death of Christopher Marlowe in Deptford four years earlier.

This was the first of many skirmishes with the authorities. In 1603 his tragedy *Sejanus* was denounced to the Council for 'popery and treason', and in 1605 he was in prison again, for the comedy *Eastward Ho,* co-written with George Chapman and John Marston. The trouble this time was a joke—'I ken the man weel: he's one of my thirty pound knights'—which hit too obviously at King James's sale of honours. Punishment for this sort of thing was no joke. When the authors were arrested, 'the report was that they should then have their ears cut, and noses.'

Confrontation was Jonson's mode as a man and a writer. He was a fighter. His literary quarrels often spilled over into physical violence: he 'beat' his colleague Marston and 'took his pistol from him', and in 1598, he killed the actor Gabriel Spenser in a sword fight on Hoxton Fields. This resulted in another spell in prison, and nearly the gallows for manslaughter. While in prison he converted to Catholicism: another confrontation. For 12 years he and his wife Anne suffered the fines and petty recriminations of recusancy. In 1610 he returned to the Anglican fold and 'at his first communion, in token of true reconciliation, he drank out all the full cup of wine': a typical Jonson gesture.

Sometimes the confrontation seems like truculence, literary machismo: a 17th-century Hemingway. Sometimes he mocks it in himself. But in the end it is his particular gift. Riggs champions that 'powerfully subversive streak' in him. There is courage and isolation in Jonson's story, the 'plain-speaker' in an age of political concealment. He 'comes near to us not as a father or a judge, but as a chronic transgressor who lived to tell the tale'. The price he paid for this can be seen in his turbulent life, and in the eyes of his portrait. His own motto, handwritten in his books, was from Seneca: *Tamquam Explorator*. That was how he valued himself, 'as an explorer'.

a curious life

THAT TIRELESS scribbler John Aubrey died suddenly, aged 71, sometime during the first week of June 1697. His funeral was held at St Mary Magdalen church in Oxford 300 years ago today. The parish register records: 'John Aubery a stranger was buryed Jun 7th.'

The term 'stranger' means merely that he was not of the parish—he lived all his life in the Wiltshire hamlet of Easton Piers, near Malmesbury—but it carries a certain resonance of the man. Aubrey never quite belonged: he was an observer more than a participant. In academic circles he was a marginal, quirky figure, and he remains so in the eyes of posterity. He spent a lifetime recording 'curiosities' of all sorts, and is now

Weekend Telegraph, 1997

considered something of a curiosity himself. The range of his interests defies classification—biographer, topographer, antiquary, mathematician, folklorist, archaeologist: the list could go on. He is sometimes described as a 'miscellanist', a term redolent of a bygone age of genial scholarly browsing. This is partly right, but does not catch Aubrey's out-and-about quality—was 'never off horseback'—nor his reportorial relish for gossip and raciness. Contemporaries described him variously as a 'learned honest gentleman', a 'professed virtuoso, always replete with new discoveries', and a 'shiftless person, roving and maggoty-headed'.

There is a memorial plaque on the west wall of St Mary Magdalen, put there in the 1980s, but his true monument lies a few hundred yards away at the Bodleian Library. It is a monument of paper—50 assorted leatherbound volumes of his manuscripts and letters, packed with his small, rapid, slightly obsessive handwriting. Leafing through these cluttered pages, abuzz with addenda and marginalia, with doodles and diagrams, you seem almost to be looking into his mind.

AUBREY IS best know for his marvellous collection of biographical sketches, *Brief Lives,* of which he said: 'These remaines are *tamquam tabulata naufragi* [like the fragments of a shipwreck] that after the Revolution of so many years and governments have escaped the teeth of time.' This catches the nature of their perennial appeal. Jotted down over decades, unpublished until 1813—and then only in very bowdlerised form—the *Lives* are a gold mine for the historian. They are full of rackety details and contemporary gossip, of irresistible if usually unverifiable anecdotes—Sir Walter Ralegh 'getting up one of the Maids of Honour up against a tree'; Ben Jonson drinking canary wine in an old 'coachman's coat, with slits under the armpits', and so on.

Equally piquant are the many minor, forgotten figures who appear in its pages—Dr Willis, who had 'dark brindle hair like a red pig' and 'stammered much'; Sir Jonas Moore, who 'cured his sciatica by boiling his buttock'. Here is the brief life of Dr Richard Stokes:

> Scholar to Mr William Oughtred for Mathematiques (Algebra). Made himself mad with it, but became sober again, but I feare like a crackt glasse. Became Roman Catholique. Married unhappily at Liège, dog and catt, etc. Became a sott. Dyed in Newgate, prisoner for debt, April 1681.

Aubrey is the master of biographical compression (something today's 800-page merchants could learn from) and the cryptic but suggestive aside. Apropos the Countess of Kent, 'I remember in 1646 or 1647 they did talk also of my Lady's she-blackamoor.' He had a nose for salacious stories about the great and good. Mistress Overall, wife of the Dean of St Paul's, was discovered *in flagrante,* lying 'upon Sir John Selby's bed as flat as any flounder'. The Countess of Pembroke—Sir Philip Sidney's sister—had a 'videtto' or peep-hole made for her at Wilton House so she could watch the stallions 'leape the mares' and then 'act the like sport herself with her stallions'. (In the manuscript this passage is scored out, apparently by Aubrey himself, though not enough to make it illegible.)

The *Lives* are an accretion of notes rather than a finished work. They were 'set down tumultuarily', he said, 'as if tumbled out of a sack'. Oliver Lawson Dick, whose excellent edition appeared in 1949 (and who sadly died in his mid-forties in 1964), reckoned the total number of lives as 426. But some are merely copied from other sources, and some take brevity too far—Aubrey's life of John Holywood consists of a single sentence: 'Dr Pell is positive that his name was Holybushe.' Lawson Dick stitched together 136 lives out of this Aubreian 'gallimaufry' of fact and anecdote.

The lack of method seems now a positive quality. The *Lives* have a rawness and intimacy. He compared the biographer to a 'conjuror' who 'makes them walk and appear that have layen in their graves many hundreds of years.' One catches too a sense of Aubrey himself, the inquisitor at large. Scattered through the manuscripts is the word *Quaere,* or simply Q—a memo to himself to ask someone something. '*Quaere* Dr Pell, what is the use of those inverted logarithmes?', '*Quaere* whether there are mussel-shells in the Thames', and so on. He was the great inquirer, the pursuivant of fugitive details. His interviewees sometimes found him tiresome. Dr John Newton 'told me he was borne in Bedfordshire, but would not tell me where'. And 'the Earl of Carnarvon does not remember Mr Brown; I ask't his Lordship lately if any of his servants do; he assures me NO.'

The chaos of the Civil War made Aubrey acutely aware of

the precariousness of historical remembrance. He woke up in a cold sweat thinking of all those interesting old parchments used to wrap herrings and stop mustard-pots. He rescued a rich stratum of oral history about the Elizabethans, of whom our personal knowledge is scant. He quizzed a dying generation of eyewitnesses and childhood reminiscencers. (He was to the Elizabethans, chronologically, as we are to the Edwardians.) In London, in the old theatrical quarter of Shoreditch, he found a grandson of Shakespeare's colleague Christopher Beeston; another old-stager called Lacey supplied him with memories of Ben Jonson. He tapped into the Ralegh family via Sir Walter's great-nephews, who were at school with him.

AUBREY'S OWN life is less well known, outwardly uneventful but rich in charm and curiosity. He records its small dramas— mortgages, lawsuits, bungled courtships, hawking trips—with the nonchalant irony that marks the *Lives*: 'This yeare [1666] all my businesses and affaires ran kim-kam.'

The son of a minor Wiltshire squire, he was a sickly, studious child, prone to agues and colics, 'mild of spirit' and 'mightily susceptible of fascination'. His 'phansie' or imagination was 'like pure chrystal water which the least wind does disorder and unsmoothe'. He grew up in a secluded farmhouse, looking out over the 'thin blew lanskape' of Wiltshire, walking river-banks riotous with 'calver-keys, hare-parsley, wild vetch, maiden's honesty, polypodium, foxgloves, wild vine, bayle, and many vulnerary plants now by me forgot'.

He studied at Trinity College, Oxford, but the outbreak of war in 1642 forced him home. He was torn between gregariousness and seclusion. He never married, though there were doomed alliances, most notably with Joan Sumner, to whom 'I made my first addresse, in an ill-howre' in 1665. Little is known of the relationship. That she told him of a recipe used by thieves to stop dogs barking—a mixture of boar's fat and cumin seeds—is pungent if not quite romantic. It ended in lawsuits, 'opprobrious speeches', and the embarrassment of an arrest on Chancery Lane.

An expressive pen-and-ink portrait by William Faithorne shows Aubrey in 1666, at the age of 40. He has big eyes and a thin moustache. It is a very likeable face, but has an unexpected air of uncertainty or even bitterness.

The following year Aubrey met the irascible Oxford don and gossip, Anthony Wood. They spent 3s 8d drinking 'at Mother Web's'. Wood writes: 'Mr Aubrey was then in a sparkish garb, came to town with his man and two horses, spent high, and flung out A. W. at all reckonings.' It was the caustic Wood who described Aubrey as 'maggoty-headed'. He complained that Aubrey fed him 'fooleries and misinformations', but this is sour considering how much of Aubrey's research he used, without acknowledgement, for his own biographical collections, *Athenae Oxonienses* (1691-2).

Aubrey's most measurable achievement was as a founder member of the Royal Society. He was a great experimenter. One hundred years before the first manned balloon flight he wrote: 'Fill or force in smoke into a bladder, and try if the bladder will not be carried up in the ayre, if it is so, several bladders may draw a man up into the ayre a certain height.' He was also a pioneering archaeologist. He discovered the ancient stone-ring at Avebury. He wrote brilliantly about places as well as people. (Having grown up in Surrey county, I have a soft spot for his neglected *Perambulation of Surrey*, last published in 1719.)

His only work to be published in his lifetime was simply called *Miscellanies* (1696). A grab-bag of superstitions and occultisms, it is largely unreadable—may even be, as the learned cleric Dr Stratford described it, 'a mad book'—but the title is apt for his maverick eclecticism. Aubrey's genius lies precisely in his dilettantism, in his capturing of the diverse and ephemeral, the common currency, the lightweight truths of an age: 'cookery, chemistry, cards'. His manuscripts contain a world, lovingly observed and preserved amid the upheavals of war. The historian G. M. Young sums him up eloquently: 'Across this shifting landscape he flits, noticing everything'.

His last dateable note was written on 1 June 1697—a memo to the bookseller Awnsham Churchill, directing his attention to 'a very pretty remarque concerning apparitions' in the *Athenian Mercury*. He hopes it can be inserted into the next edition of *Miscellanies*. He gives the exact volume, number and date. The precision is with him to the end, and the enthusiasm, and the poignant overtone of pointlessness.

He once described himself as 'surprised with age', and he was probably surprised with death as well; at any rate, he died intestate. It was perhaps a recurrence of the 'apoplexy' or stroke which he had suffered three years earlier. An air of surprise attends his whole life: everything is so curious, so puzzling, so worthy of 'remarque', and down it goes into the notebook whose pages one opens up today, as if uncorking an old dusty phial marked 'Tonick' and finding the contents still fresh and full of zest.

wild, manly, whistling

'AH WELL,' said the taxi driver, when he learned this was my first visit to Dublin. 'You never saw the city as it was, but you'll see it as it is.'

In the sombre light of an April afternoon, Dublin as it is seems disappointingly familiar. First the grid of grey housing-estate roofs: Ballymun and Santry. Then the dowdy frontages of Drumcondra Road: pushchairs and plastic headscarves, greengrocers and funeral parlours, red-brick terraces leading off. It could be Kilburn. It could be Glasgow. It could be some half-remembered High Street from the 1950s. The driver grumbles about the state of the roads: they are laying new gas-pipes throughout the city. On a wall I see written, 'THE SHIP

Departures 1988

IS SINKING BUT WE WON'T DROWN'. Then we're into O'Connell Street, wider and grander: monuments to Parnell and Jim Larkin, the Post Office with its bullet-pocked columns, Clery's department store, the Gresham Hotel where Marlene Dietrich and Ronald Reagan rub shoulders in the guest-book. Rain spatters the windscreen. The umbrellas go up: office girls' dainty foldaways, businessmen's black brollies, striped golf umbrellas bearing the logos of Sony, Irish Life and the Millennium. 'And there isn't Nelson's Column,' says the driver. (It was reduced to rubble by a Republican bomb in 1966, the fiftieth anniversary of the Easter Rising.) At a work-site in the middle of the street a new monument is being built. Another great reformer or Republican hero? No: a fountain in honour of the late Jefferson Smurfitt, founder of Ireland's giant paper and packaging empire.

We cross O'Connell Bridge. The Liffey is sullen and dark, its sheer stone embankments are black, and the clouds seem to reach down and touch the arched back of the Ha'penny Bridge just downriver.

In an hour's time the colour of the river will be different—still grey, perhaps, but a different grey—and on the Northside quays in the early morning, with the sun slanting in over Pigeon House chimneys, across the roofs of Ringsend, past the motionless dockyard cranes, you will see the water lit up a deep, turbid green. But you don't know about that yet. Dublin is a city of moods. It hides its charms behind a shabby exterior, 'the coat so old and the light in the head', and you must be a little patient, slip down a gear or two, before it starts to work on you.

THE SHELBOURNE Hotel is pure pickled Dublin as it was. Even the porters wear tweed jackets. Outside the portico, flanked by luciferous Nubian statues, Jimmy Corcoran the doorman is dispensing weather-wise advice to comers and goers. In the lobby a party of elderly American golfers mingles with a few lost liggers left over from the Eurovision Song Contest.

The Shelbourne's grand façade, 'tall as a cliff but more genial' in the words of Elizabeth Bowen, looks down over Stephen's Green, the largest garden square in Europe. The chestnuts and planes are already in leaf. There are bandstands and duckponds, and a garden for the blind with tactile plants and botanical names in Braille. The Green is a hub for the easy pleasures of the Southside—shopper's Dublin down Grafton Street, clubber's Dublin down Leeson Street, bespoke pubs like O'Donoghue's and Toner's down Baggot Street, and the surviving remnants of Georgian Dublin in little pockets all around. Beyond the trees of the Green you look over to the changing colours of the Dublin mountains. It is one of the pleasures of Dublin that you are never far away from natural beauty. A short ride by car will take you up into the hills, or out into the green pastures of County Kildare, and a short ride along the DART trainline will take you to the sea: to the weather-beaten fishing town of Howth on the northern tip of the bay, to the pretty

harbour of Dun Laoghaire, to quiet Sandycove where hale oc-
togenarians bathe naked in the Forty Foot Pool, just as 'stately,
plump Buck Mulligan' does at the beginning of *Ulysses*.

YOU SOON come to realise that Dublin is just what the song
promised, a 'fair' city, but you cannot help wondering how
long it will remain so. Planners, speculators and good old Irish
indifference have disfigured the city. Tracts of Georgian Dublin
are still being levelled to the ground. Even on Upper Merrion
Street, right opposite Leinster House, there's a terrace waiting
for the chop, the fanlights all broken, the tall sash windows
boarded up. A classic example of planner's blight is Wood
Quay, where Dublin Corporation has built an office-block of
surpassing banality right in the lee of Christ Church Cathedral,
covering up as they did so a rich cache of Viking remains.
People say: if the Corporation got away with that, they can get
away with anything. People will also tell you that it isn't just
architecture that's suffered. The old populous heart of the city
has been torn out, rehoused, traffic-planned. With it has gone
something of the compactness and intimacy which were once
Dublin's special hallmark. Sixty-five years ago, at the time of
Independence, metropolitan Dublin covered the area between
the Royal and Grand Canals, and along the east coast to Dun
Laoghaire. Since then it has grown sixfold in size, stretching
from the mountains in the south to the airport in the north,
from the coast to the bleak satellites of Tallaght and Blan-
chardstown. The Corporation's latest development plan speaks

ominously of further 'rejuvenation'—i.e., depopulation—for traditional working-class areas like the Liberties, the Quays and Smithfield. The docklands are being systematically tarted up along the lines of London. At Custom House Dock, a stone's throw from the remnants of the old dockland community along Sheriff Street and Gardiner Street, they are preparing to build a 'major international financial centre', which will also contain two hundred luxury apartments, a marina and a heliport.

Battles have been lost, but others are now being fought more keenly by groups like An Taisce: a road scheme called the Inner Tangent, described by locals as 'The Road to God Knows Where'; a dual carriageway through Harold's Cross; the conversion of the Royal Dublin Society show ground in Ballsbridge to offices; and a marina complex at Dun Laoghaire which has embroiled Charlie Haughey, not for the first time, in accusations of being hand-in-glove with the speculators.

'**BOOM-TOWN** politics,' says Liam *à propos* all of this, 'but where's the focking boom?'

Liam Corless: a dark man in his forties, a musician by vocation, but meanwhile keeping body and soul together as a repairman for a TV-rental shop in Phibsborough. I met him in a pub called the Cross Guns, set between the black waters of the Royal Canal and the grey barbed walls of Mountjoy Prison. He was drinking Guinness with a glass of Bush on the side, 'a little bit of the cream and a little bit of the bite'.

It soon transpired that Liam was a *rale Dub*. With all this dispersal, a 'real' Dubliner is as elusive as a real Cockney in London. Liam's family now lives in a semi in Ballymun, but he was born and brought up in the old back-to-backs of the Liberties. This in itself qualified him for real Dubdom. The Liberties run west of the cathedrals, outside the old town walls, hence the name. The area is now much depleted—some of it gentrified, some of it demolished and replaced with half-deserted moonscapes of brick, graffiti and dismembered vehicles—but in parts you can catch a little of the old flavour: bustling clothes markets and bric-a-brac stalls, smoke coming from the chimneys, turfs of peat on sale at corner shops. The walls no longer smell, as they once did, of 'pig's cheek and cabbage', but you can still smell the ubiquitous Irish 'fry' on the stove if you stroll the streets on a Sunday lunchtime.

Liam learned to love music lying in his bed as a child, listening to the ballads floating out from the Capstan Bar on New Row. Now, did I know that once in times gone by the pub was owned by the legendary boxer Dan Donnelly? And that Donnelly's arms were so long he could button his breeches at the knees without stooping? And that one of his arms can be seen in a glass case at a pub called the Hideout in Kilcullen, though verification of its extreme length is not possible because it is 'said to be now much shrunken'? This reminded me I had not yet visited St Michan's to shake the crusader's hand. A treat in store: shaking the crusader's hand, I was told, felt like grasping the foot of a giant chicken.

Over a third of Ireland's population lives in Dublin, and a Dub will tell you that the city is packed full of 'kulchies' (people up from the country: the word derives from Kiltimagh, a small town in County Mayo), not to mention American tourists, Oriental students, and Euro-businessmen hanging on to the rapidly fraying coat-tails of Ireland's post-EEC expansion.

'But a Dub,' Liam conceded, 'is just a kulchie who's been here longer.' His grandfather came from Galway, from a little village on the coast, 'next stop New York'. Liam had dark eyes, thinning black hair swept back. His Dublin pallor—rain, greasy food, pub smoke—was set over a more swarthy complexion. (His clothes were black too: nothing 'dandy' about Liam, a word he used with pejorative overtones.) He looked vaguely Mediterranean, I thought, and indeed he told me that, according to family tradition, the Corlesses are descended from a shipwrecked Armada sailor called Carlos. It was Friday afternoon, the holy hour just finished, and Liam was in celebratory mood having won tidily at the dogs at Shelbourne Park last night. 'Pig or harp?' he said. This is Irish for heads or tails, these being the emblems on the 5*p* coin. Pigs, and Liam would return to work at the TV shop. Harps, and he would gather a few of his friends up, and 'go for a bit of crack [partying] on the Southside.'

He tossed the coin. It came up harps. In Dublin it so often does.

I NEVER heard Liam play the uillean pipes, but I heard plenty of music: rock music and traditional music, Hothouse Flowers and Comhaltas Ceoltori, electric guitars and penny-whistles. My memories of Dublin are set to music, in a soundtrack entwined with other Dublin sounds: seagulls on a raid over the Green, tinkers' horses fast-trotting down the street, the calling of the fruitsellers down Moore Street and Mary Street.

The most famous spot for pub music is O'Donoghue's— most nights you can hardly get in through the doors, and the first thing you see, above the close-packed heads, is a barman crouched up above the bar like some gladiatorial warrior, taking the shouted orders from halfway across the room—but better I remember a nothing-much pub on the South Circular Road at Sunday lunchtime, the band drifting in from the twelve o'clock mass, nursing their Saturday night heads, tuning up their instruments—fiddle, accordion, pipes and bodhran— and moving into a melancholy jaunty jig called 'My Love He Came To Dublin Town'. But you don't need to go to a pub to hear live music. Walking down Grafton Street, on your way to take coffee at Bewley's, you'll hear half-a-dozen buskers in a couple of hundred yards, including the venerable Lord Mustard, with long white moustache and clown's suit, dancing to the tune of 'Consider Yourself' on his little ghetto-blaster. And on a stormy holiday Monday, on the waterfront at Howth, a trio was playing down-home skiffle, as the wind moaned plaintively into the microphone between the singer's lines.

Street music and balladry hold a special place in Dublin's heart. On College Street there's a statue to the balladeer Tom Moore, its proximity to the public conveniences giving rise to puns on his famous lyric, 'The Meeting of the Waters'. In Glasnevin cemetery, a monument is dedicated to the blind ballad-singer Michael Moran, known as Zozimus. He is remembered for songs such as 'In Egypt's Land', in which the Pharaoh's daughter discovers the infant Moses in the rushes and cries, 'Tarranagers, girls, which of yez owns the child?' When Zozimus died in 1846, the city's ballad singers converged on his dingy lodgings on Patrick Street, and held a wake the like of which the city hasn't heard since. Another wake, another jig—

> *Wasn't it truth I told you,*
> *Lots of fun at Finnegan's Wake*

—gave Joyce the title for his last impenetrable masterpiece. Joyce himself had a fine tenor voice, and would often sing his favourite ballad, 'The Brown and Yellow Ale'. During their years of exile in Europe, his wife Nora was heard to remark that 'Jim should have stuck to the singing.'

There was a political bite to the tradition of street-singing, and perhaps this lingers in the political commitment of latter-day Dublin rockers like Bob Geldof and U2's Bono. Some have liked them less since they became millionares, but U2 is still *the* Dublin band. Down among the eerie quiet quays on the Southside, at the Windmill Lane studios where the band records, there's a wall filled with the scrawled messages of teenage devotion: 'NOW AT LAST I AM HOME—SYLVIA', and 'BONO: THANKS FOR THE STRENGTH—YVONNE', and (more modestly) 'BONO: THANKS FOR GETTING OUT OF THE MINIBUS'.

★   ★   ★

THE REST of the soundtrack is voices. Talk is up there with music in the Dublin world-view, and the extraordinary richness of the city's literary tradition is a kind of distillation of this. Swift, Wilde, Yeats, Synge, Shaw, Joyce, O'Casey and Beckett all have their corner somewhere in the city, but the literary flavour that lingers most strongly is the bohemian Dublin of the post-war years, the roaring world of writers like Brendan Behan, Patrick Kavanagh and Brian O'Nolan (a.k.a. Flann O'Brien and Myles na Gopaleen). They are all three dead now, but one who hunted with that pack, and is still very much extant, is the poet Anthony Cronin.

He's in his early 60s, a small man in corduroys and tortoise-shell specs, with a big domed forehead beneath a raffish cloth cap, rather like the one in the famous portrait of the young Joyce, with his hands in his pockets and his head on one side and his shadowed quizzical eyes looking out at the photographer (wondering, he later admitted, 'would he lend me five shillings'.)

Cronin has a quieter, more donnish air than I expected. There's the ghost of a florid complexion, recalling the carouses of yesteryear, but when I ask him what will he be having, he wistfully orders a Perrier. He says, 'It got to the point where the things that happened because of the drink began to be outweighed by the things that *didn't* happen because of the drink.' He had seen too many good men when 'the whiskey had become the master and was cracking the whip.'

He is eminently respectable now: official biographer of

Flann O'Brien, contributor to the Bloomsday celebrations, dweller on Westland Row, and cultural adviser—'keeping a corner for art and literature'—to the Taoiseach. Literature, he feels, has 'come in from the cold', become a part of the mainstream of Dublin life. That bohemian world of the 1950s, though convivial, was 'born out of a kind of political despair'. To be a writer then, he says, 'meant that you were on the outside. You saw no point in politics. You had no common interest with society. Nowadays writers are conscious of themselves as a lobby. They identify with certain social movements. They come out of the universities—not just the university of the gutter, like us.'

He affectionately recalls the mammoth poverty of their lives: 'We knew not what the day would bring. We lived the law of desperate circumstances, which is that if you're in them you'll make them worse.'

One of his closest friends was the poet Patrick Kavanagh, author of 'The Great Hunger' and 'Kitty Stobling' and the exquisite air 'On Raglan Road'. Another kulchie—he was from Monaghan up near the Ulster border—Kavanagh seems now the quintessence of the Dublin poet, a big, shambling, bespectacled man, a king whose court was the pub, the bookies, the small magazine, the slim volume. Cronin remembers him in his lodgings on Pembroke Road, boiling up an egg in the teapot for his supper. He took out cups of tea to the workmen as they dug up the road outside to disconnect his unpaid-for electricity.

And later, in the dark days of chronic alcoholism: 'He kept a bottle of whiskey under his pillow, and he would actually drink from it without appearing to wake up, as a baby does.' Cronin was also the friend of the brawling Dublin wit Brendan Behan. Born in the dockside slums, educated at Borstal, imprisoned as a member of the IRA, Behan finally turned his chequered past to good account in plays like *The Quare Fellow* and *The Hostage*. These brought him brief fame and fortune before he died in 1964, burned out at the age of forty. He is buried in the Prospect cemetery at Glasnevin, where the inscription reads: *'File, fiáin, feadánach'*—'wild, manly, whistling'.

Cronin says, 'I perhaps knew the others more closely, but I think I regret Brendan more keenly.'

Regret for so much that remained unachieved?

'Just regret that he's no longer here with us. Brendan's decline and death diminished the gaiety of nations.'

Their great haunt was a pub called McDaid's on Harry Street, now a shadow of its former self. The bar has been moved, so you can no longer sit in the corner where Behan composed, well-lubricated, at the typewriter he had borrowed off his cousin Jimmy Bourke. There's a sign for Budweiser in the window, and the tall blond barman sports an accent that certainly isn't real Dub, and in fact hails from Croydon. Behind the bar a squat CD plays Aztec Camera. Things have moved on. Kavanagh and Behan are just two more Dublin ghosts, and all that's left of them in McDaid's is the thick brown varnish of cigarette-tar on the ceiling.

'There's no pub life left in the literary sense,' Cronin says.

'We needed the assurance, the sense of identity, that the pub gave us. We were almost *compelled* to live out our lives in public. People don't live the café life so much now.'

OR PERHAPS it is just that the focus has shifted. Judging from the young writers I met, the city's literary voice is more and more to be heard in the unlovely outer reaches, in the rehoused Dublin. Dermot Bolger lives in Finglas, and his novel, *Night Shift,* draws on his experiences as a factory hand there. Tall, bespectacled and bearded, he looks like an etiolated Irish version of the young Allen Ginsberg. He runs a small publishing company, Raven Arts Press, from a terrace house in Phibsborough. His aim as a publisher and a writer is to reflect 'the new Ireland emerging'. He says, 'Dublin in the last thirty years has aged sixty years. It's like an aborigine taking to whiskey. Sometimes you feel that everything's falling apart, but I suppose that's why I live in Dublin. It's the emergence of something new. That's where a writer ought to be.'

Another suburb, Kilbarrack, formerly a fishermen's village, now a mixture of Corporation housing estates and privately-owned semis on the northern reaches of the DART line, is the stamping ground of Roddy Doyle, playwright and novelist. His novel *The Commitments* is about the ups and downs of a soul band in an outer Dublin suburb. They sing the James Brown classic, 'Night Train', with DART stations substituted for the American cities of the original. Doyle calls the area Barrytown, but in all but name it's Kilbarrack. It's a street-wise book, much of its slang picked up from young Kilbarrackers at the local comprehensive where Doyle teaches English and geography. 'I like teaching here,' he tells me, over a lunchtime drink in a chilly modern barn of a pub round the corner. 'School keeps me up to date. I don't snoop, but I keep my ear open for what's happening with the kids. In the media, Dublin has been strangely ignored. On RTE you'll hear every Irish accent there is, but never a regular Dubliner. We're still stuck in this phoney rural image of Ireland.'

The mood of these writers, both under thirty, is felt also in the work of young film-makers like Neil Jordan and Aisling Walsh. They want to leave the blarney behind, and deal with the pressing realities of urban Ireland, Dublin as it is.

Those realities are often harsh ones. One in five of the city's working population is unemployed: in places like Finglas and Ballymun, unemployment is up to 70 per cent. 'The kids in Ballymun are second-generation unemployed,' says Liam. 'Unemployment is as natural to them as the rain. Wait until you're eighteen for the welfare. Then draw the welfare until you're old enough for a pension.' The city's drug statistics tell the same story: an estimated 3000 heroin addicts in a city of a million, and this despite a high price of £150 per gram. (The price is high because in trafficking terms Dublin leads nowhere: it is a cul-de-sac rather than a transit-point.) Increasing severity in the courts has, predictably, had little effect. Addiction—says James Comberton, chairman of Coolemine House, Dublin's only full-time therapeutic community—is a 'failure of identity', an ethic of 'kids born to fail'. There are beggars in the streets, often young women with a child or two in tow, rattling an ice-cream tub full of coppers. They look like country girls in their tattered shawls and ankle-socks. The Irish give generously: charity is in their nature.

One night in the lashing rain I share an awning with a woman so swaddled in coats and scarves that she looks like Giles's granny, but when the light from a passing car falls on her face I see the tubby features of a girl in her late teens. Her name is Mary. Her family is in Donegal. She's half-simple. I ask her why has she come to Dublin, where will she sleep tonight. She doesn't answer, instead asks me to buy her a gravy and chips at the chippie. I figure this is more useful to her than questions. She takes the little package, shuffles off into the rain, past the giant modern statue of Wolfe Tone, heading for her cardboard box in a doorway off Grafton Street.

The slow rhythms of Dublin—entirely tonic to the visitor— hint also at stagnation and despair. The name Dublin is from the Gaelic *dubh linn,* which means 'black pool', and sometimes you seem to see down through the charm of the place, down through its subtle garrulous gaiety, to the darkness underneath.

THE PUB may no longer be the literary forum it was in Anthony Cronin's day, but it is still the focal point of Dublin life. There are 834 pubs in Dublin City and County, and the city's drinkers spend £1 million a day on Guinness alone. 'The pub to a Dub,' says Liam, 'is like an oasis to a Bedouin. It's just that we don't like to walk so far in between.' There are many reasons put forward for the superiority of Irish Guinness over the ersatz brew served up in Britain. You will hear it ascribed to the correctness of the temperature (9 to 11 degrees optimum), the regular maintenance of the cooling pipes, the arcane mysteries of barmanship (such as always leaving the glass three-quarters full for a minute or two, before the pale junkety head is added). Each pub's pint is tested and tasted with a wine buff's acumen. The best tastes, as Liam puts it, 'like God in velvet trousers'.

'Will you be having another one, then?'

'Sure and a bird can't fly on one wing.'

And then, when the pubs finally empty out around quarter to midnight, when the city takes on its faintly East European air of desertion and wet pavements, there's nowhere much else to go except back home, or to Leeson Street. By day the area round Leeson Street is a brass-plaque world of accountants, architects and private clinics. The shuttered clubs in the basements are all but invisible. But at night, they blossom into a winking foot-level flora of neon—Legg's, Fanny Hill's, Maxwell Plum's, Styx, Samantha's. At Buck Whaley's it's 'regulars only' tonight, which Liam informs me is because I'm wearing jeans and sneakers, so we go to Von B's: champagne at £20 a bottle, cranked-up disco music, a dance floor the size of a ping-pong table, a leggy girl at the bar wearing a leopard-skin print dress and half an ounce of makeup. There's a general air of dodgy opulence about the men—didn't I see that fat guy with the cigar down at the Raffles-style bar in Sach's Hotel a couple of days ago?—and an air of negotiable virtue about the women.

It isn't the Kips or Monto—the old red-light districts around the docks, Joyce's Nighttown: 'Night hides her body's flaws, calling under her brown shawl from an archway where dogs have mired'—but there are a few brassers around in the clubs, and plenty more patrolling the kerb in twos and threes down Fitzwilliam Street, or round the church called the Pepper Cannister.

And when the clubs in turn disgorge their human cargo, and it's definitely too late to stop now, you can stroll on down to the Grand Canal. From Leeson Street Bridge, you can walk either way—upstream towards Dolphin Barn, or east towards the eerie cobbled streets and dark dripping tunnels around Grand Canal Dock—or, if not, you can cross over the bridge and round the night off at Ruth Roberts' All Night Café, where the music plays neither too loud nor too soft.

The Grand Canal crosses half the country, linking the Shannon with Dublin Bay, 'bringing from Athy and other farflung towns mythologies'. Here it is a haven of shady walks, lovers' benches, wild valerian growing out of the rubble, tangled gardens leading down to the water's edge. In the night there are water-rats rustling in the reeds, and a heron that played a kind of grandmother's footsteps with me all the way up to Baggot' Street Bridge.

By Baggot Street Bridge one afternoon I sat on the bench put there in memory of Patrick Kavanagh. The canal was his great haunt. His fine poem is carved in the granite: 'O commemorate me where there is water'. I felt I was beginning to understand why it was that Kavanagh called Dublin 'the cruellest city on the face of the earth'. Dublin is cruel, he said, because it leads you on. 'A city should ignore you, like London does, which gives you the English cold shoulder. But Dublin is full of warm promises, like the worst sort of woman.'

The afternoon was close and hazy, but the man sitting on the grass a few feet away was wrapped in a dirty serge overcoat. He was a big red-faced man with a bristling salt-and-pepper beard. He was drinking from a bottle of cheap sherry, and—there was no pretending otherwise—he was waving me over to talk to him.

He spoke with a rasp: 'I want you to read me something.'

I thought he meant the poem on Paddy Kavanagh's bench, but now he was clambering to his feet and beckoning me to follow: past the bench, towards the roar of the lock below the bridge, to a mooring-post, a wooden pile painted black and white, angled away from the bank. He crouched down and cleared away the tufts of grass and stitchwort that grew around the base. There I saw a little tin cross, and the words written beneath it, ink under plastic: 'IN LOVING MEMORY OF JOHNNY AND FRANCIS McCANN, DROWNED HERE ON 8-9TH AUGUST 1984.'

The red-faced man was Gerry McCann, their elder brother. They had all three come to Dublin from County Mayo in 1951. On that August night they had been drinking hard, down at O'Brien's just off Leeson Street. Johnny, the youngest, fell into the lock. Frank jumped in to try and save him.

Gerry McCann came here often now. He had made the little tin cross himself, but he had to get someone else to write the words—and passers-by like me, from time to time, to read them to him. He knew what they said, of course, but he liked 'to hear it done properly'. Despite having come here for four years he was quite ignorant of the poet's words on the nearby bench. He stood up, swayed beside the lock, looked down at the bobbing detritus of beer cans and burger trays. He beckoned me over with his bottle-hand. I was reluctant to stand so near the water, reluctant to take the proffered slug of sherry, but it seemed churlish not to. This is my Dublin moment: the rank sweetness of the bottle, the black waters of the lock, the company of a tramp and a dead poet. Then the moment passes, and Gerry McCann turns away from the lock, muttering words I can't understand.

incident at yaviza

THE PEOPLE of Panama elect a new president on 7 May. The loudspeaker vans are cruising the streets, the spray cans are at work on the walls, but the heart of it is dead. Whatever the outcome of the elections, everyone knows that the real power will continue to be held by the military, under the command of General Manuel Antonio ('Tony') Noriega.

The soldiers are everywhere. The 16,000-strong Fuerzas de Defensa, the National Guard, the gun-toting police: the various uniforms blur into one nervous presence. The people are used to it, philosophical about the pyramid of military power and profiteering on which Noriega sits. It is said that every time you pay a $10 bribe to a highway cop, Tony gets 80 cents.

Independent, 1990

He seems more powerful than ever. Last year the United States indicted him for drug-trafficking, and tried to freeze him from power by cutting off the country's currency supplies. He sat tight. In nationalist Panama they'll forgive you a lot if you're seen to stand up to the Yankee Aggressor. 'Of course Noriega's a crook,' said a student I met in Penonomé. 'But right now he's a popular crook.'

He is also a clever one. His answer to the drug indictments has been a series of veiled countercharges. He recalls his former collaborations with American narcotics agencies, shows off the plaque he received in recognition of his services, and hints that he knows a thing or two about the dingier activities of the CIA in Central America. This touches a nerve with President Bush, who was director of the CIA in the mid-1970s. A former Noriega aide, Colonel Roberto Diaz Herrera, quotes him as saying: 'I have Bush by the balls.' This remark is classic Noriega neighbourhood-bully talk.

So now the dollars are back on stream, a half-hearted carnival has come and gone, and the pre-election mood in Panama City is one of heavily policed calm. The calm is partly just a silence. Independent television and radio stations are shut down, and the main opposition newspaper, *La Prensa*, has been closed. Noriega has promised to lift the ban in time for the elections, but there's no sign of this. The only national daily is *La Estrella de Panama,* a thin production that reeks of official sanitisation.

Real opposition is risky. More than 50 politicians and journalists are now in jail, many others in exile. On the graffiti-covered sea-walls of Panama City, you still see the name of Dr Hugo Spadafora, an old foe of Noriega. His headless body was found just across the frontier in Costa Rica. The story was put around that Spadafora was killed by Salvadorean guerrillas, but no one pretends to believe this.

TO THIS general picture of martial law, I have a personal footnote to add. I recently visited Panama, together with the photographer Tim Page. It was a rather brief visit, for reasons that will become clear, but it brought us face to face—very nearly boot to teeth—with the political realities of Panama.

Our assignment was on the crazy side, but entirely nonpolitical. We were going to walk through the Darién Gap. This is a dense tract of jungle, mountain and mosquito-swamp stretching across the frontier between Panama and Colombia. There are no roads down there: you can hire the odd ride in an Indian dugout, but the rest of the time you walk. If you're fit, you can cross the Gap in a week. We expected to take two.

We planned to travel down to the Darién by cargo-boat from Panama City—20 hours in primitive conditions, hence good copy. But the carnival was under way, and no boats were sailing from the vulture-haunted wharfs of the Muelle Fiscal. We decided we'd do a quick 'recon'—the term was Page's— by road. We would check out the terrain, get some local information, maybe even sign up a local Chocó to carry our backpacks when we returned. There was also a perverse fascination in riding to the end of one of the world's great roads, the Pan-American Highway. It runs southwest of Panama City for 150 miles, dwindles from blacktop to laterite to dirt road, and then disappears for the entire length of the Darién Gap, before re-emerging in the Colombian Andes.

We hired a four-wheel-drive Nissan Patrol, Tim strapped on his Leicas, and we set off for the small jungle town of Yaviza at the end of the line.

After an hour or so, you're down to maximum practical speed of 25 mph. You go in a serpentine pattern, avoiding the holes by following local tyre-tracks. Frequent rivers are crossed via alarming little Bailey bridges with a metal track for each wheel and open space between them. We lunched at a small road-house: fish, rice and beans. A logger in a check shirt and green canvas jungle boots was eating on the verandah. Logging in the Darién is tightly controlled, but with a few *mordidas* (bribes) here and there, a living is possible. He complained of the irony of the logging quotas. 'There are maybe 60 loggers working down here,' he said. 'But there's 1,000 settlers along the road, and they're allowed to burn the forest to the ground.'

We asked him why there was still no road through the Darién. He said that international money had been put up for the project, but—he tapped his wallet-pocket—'the money never got here.' Did he mean it was pocketed by Noriega and his cronies? He wouldn't say. Even down here you're unwise to complain too loudly. If you do, you're liable to lose the government loans on which every smallholder depends. Since February, the country's $50 million agricultural credit-fund is controlled and administered by the newly created Banco Institucional de la Patria—president of the board of directors: General Noriega.

We drove on. The flat land either side of the road is cleared—scrub grass, block shacks, lonely etiolated trees—but the distant ridges are jungle. Frontier technology is much in evidence: beat-up old D8 tyres, dozers and graders, chain-saw concessions. The village signboards are all sponsored by Marlboro.

An afternoon depression settled over us. I ascribed it to the landscape: the meagreness that replaces the richness of the forest. Tim said it was the light: flat and dull, a faint clouding like steam on a windowpane.

On the outskirts of Cañazas there was a military checkpoint. We were challenged. We explained our mission: two loco gringos off to look at the Darién. We flourished letters of introduction. They took our details, and waved us on. Shortly afterwards we crossed the state-line into Darién province, which covers more than a quarter of Panama and has a population of just 30,000, about three per square mile.

We arrived at Yaviza at about 6 pm. The streets—the last gasp of the Pan-American Highway—were narrow concrete strips just wide enough for the Nissan. Yaviza is a typical tin-roofed jungle town set on the banks of the Tuira River. The population is mainly black, which gives the place a half-African air. The people were out strolling, or taking the air on rickety balconies. In a clearing near the river a basketball game was in progress.

We were directed to the town's only hotel, Los Tres Americas: a general store-cum-restaurant with a row of rooms out back, $12 a night. The room had basic furnishings, a fan, and a stand-pipe shower. After 10 hours on the road it looked fine. We planned a stroll along the riverfront, a few cold beers, and some good rest.

REST WAS the last thing we were going to get in Yaviza. We hadn't been there 10 minutes before two soldiers arrived at the hotel. They told us to accompany them to the *cuartel*: the town barracks. They implied that this was a formality—*documentación*—but their manner was surly.

At the *cuartel*, things began to take an inexorable downward turn. There were a dozen soldiers, hostile and suspicious. They had perhaps had communication from the check-point at Cañazas, and were waiting for us. This is not clear: nothing was ever made clear to us. The officer in charge was a young major, a mulatto with a fixed sneer. He wore a smart new jogging suit: maybe he had been playing in the basketball game. He took our passports, asked us a few questions. He listened unsmilingly to the answers. He nodded to a corporal, walked out, did a few press-ups and strutted off into the dusk. I thought: this isn't going to be so easy.

They put us against a wall and frisked us. They emptied out our shoulder-bags on to the table. Then we took turns to answer the corporal's questions: the full works, including names of father, mother and spouse. He typed laboriously. The proceedings were interrupted while the company mustered for flag-lowering in the parade ground: whistle-blowing, physical jerks, chants of *Viva la Patria,* a general air of low-rent goose-stepping that did little to improve our mood.

At last we signed the forms, and paid two dollars each for the privilege. We thought it might be over, but half knew it wasn't. I asked for our passports, but the corporal shook his head. We must wait, he said. They were going to radio back up the line about us. Further inquiries, *verificación.* I started to protest. The corporal told me to shut up and sit down. From that point on—though no one said so—we knew we were under arrest.

I was sent back with one of the soldiers to bring the truck round to the barracks. The rest of our equipment was hauled in. They piled our gung-ho survival gear on to the table: machetes, compasses, water-bottles. They goggled at Page's high-tech camera equipment. They scrutinised the scrawled pages of my notebook.

I am still not quite sure what, if anything, they were looking for. My guess is that first they overreacted, and thought we might actually be 'up to' something in some loco military sense. The quasi-military gear, the land cruiser stacked with tanks of reserve diesel—they didn't like it. Page had fresh Cuban visas in his passport: a Communist connection. Once you're under arrest, everything about you has a negative interpretation.

At some point they must have decided we were what we said we were: a writer and a photographer. Given the current politics, this was probably crime enough in itself. I tried to explain that ours was a travel assignment, non-political. This was outside their ken. As far as they were concerned we were dangerous snoops. It may be they had something to protect: clandestine logging interests, or the drug-run from Colombia, or some other little conduit into the Noriega pipeline.

A long period of waiting began. There were bursts of bad radio contact from time to time. We could hear some, but not all, of the conversation. I heard a voice, presumably from Cañazas, saying: 'Yes, he was taking photographs.'

It was now quite dark. Knots of soldiers lounged around the edge of the parade ground. A black woman leant in the doorway and made some assignation with the smirking corporal. The smell of the river hung in the air. This was a bad time for us. The atmosphere was malevolent. There was intimidation from two or three of the more thuggish soldiers. One caught my eye as he fingered his knife. Another, half-drunk, slapped a truncheon against his boot. There was muttered talk about *sacando la cabeza:* pulling someone's—guess whose—head off.

Empty bully talk again. As it turned out, no one laid a finger on us. But we didn't know that then. The strongest feeling was isolation: no telephones in Yaviza, just the soldiers' radio. The night was hot, the river was deep, and more than once I thought: people disappear in Panama, and this is how it happens.

It was about midnight, six hours after our detention had begun, when we at last learned our fate. We would be flown back to Panama City the next morning, to be further investigated by 'Intelligence'. We were then marched off down to the cells. A metal door, a pitch-black room, hot air laced with sweat and urine. The bolts slammed shut.

By the light of a match we saw a breeze-block room, about

10 ft by 10 ft. The only ventilation was a tiny barred window. There were six bunks, all full, and several other bodies shifting and rustling on the floor. There was scarcely room to sit, let alone sleep. No water was provided, nor sanitation. If you had to relieve yourself, you shinned up the bunks like a monkey, and pissed out between the bars of the window.

They call Panama the crossroads of the world, and one of the roads leads here.

THE CELL was awake soon after dawn. Our fellow prisoners were gentle and pleasant. They were all black, except for a Peruvian boy, an illegal immigrant. He had walked up through the Gap with little more than a toothbrush and a spare T-shirt. There was a Colombian who had been caught with a bagful of marijuana. Some local offenders were on 20-day raps for fighting and stealing.

Breakfast for 13 consisted of one mug of coffee, one dish of rock-hard plantain, and one leg of chicken. These we passed from hand to hand like a midnight feast of old.

After a while, Tim and I were led out to reclaim our bags. We were escorted off through Yaviza, which seemed to have turned out in force to watch, and down the long muddy stairs of the riverbank. We crossed the river in a dug-out with an Evinrude outboard on the back. We sat on the grass at the end of the airstrip in the morning sun, talking desultorily with our escort: one black, one a Chocó Indian, now detached from the barrack-room mob and becoming more genial.

At about 9.30 am we took off over the jungle in the local passenger plane, a twin-prop Islander. We stopped at the provincial capital, La Palma, then headed out across the Pacific, over the Pearl Islands, and into the little no-questions-asked airfield of La Paitilla in the heart of Panama City. There, five plain-clothes policemen—agents from G-2, we later learned: Counter-Intelligence, motto *Siempre Alerta*—swept us off in a red Chevy that promptly ran out of petrol on Avenida Balboa. They stood on the sidewalk waiting. We sat in the car listening to the accordions on the radio.

Metal gates opened on to the dingy yard of a building called Emigración Central. From here on, the day was an exercise in deep tedium. More questions, more laborious typewriting, more hanging around. We were not allowed to sit, or smoke, or talk unless spoken to. Otherwise we were treated with a kind of blank courtesy. At last the announcement came. We were to be deported.

We had guessed already. We were an inconvenience now, and this was the expedient solution. They made a ludicrous pretence of finding our visas out of order. It was also considered expedient to confiscate all the exposed film they could find, and my notebook.

The deportation procedure is as follows. First you must stand with your face to the wall for a few more hours. Then you are driven at great speed in the back of a panelled van to the Ministry of Justice, where your deportation order is drawn up and signed. Then you sit in reception at G-2, where there's a soft-drinks machine and Southern Command Network TV showing a tractor derby from Minneapolis. Then, just to keep you guessing, you are put in handcuffs and driven off in the red Chevy. You end up at an unmarked villa in the Bellavista district, vaguely described as Administración. Here you are shown to a barred holding-cell in the yard out back.

How long you might rot here I don't know. It was Friday night now, and it looked like a long, slow weekend. But the warders here were human. They let us send out for food, and they at last let me have the thing I had craved more than food, water or tobacco all day: a telephone.

The British Embassy in Panama, I can report, is staffed not by mere diplomats, but by angels of mercy and efficiency. It took a while, but they hung in there, shook the right hands and pulled the right strings. We walked out into the world shortly after midnight, 30 hours after our arrest at Yaviza. A little later we were sitting in deep armchairs, unshaven and evil-smelling, enjoying a gin and tonic with the ambassador, Mrs Margaret Bryant.

We were lucky. We were bullied and booted out, with a bit of petty thieving along the way, but it could have been worse. We got a glimpse of just how easy it is to get lost down there. Suddenly you've fallen into this world where you have no status, where no one needs to tell you anything, where you are not quite a person any more. That is Noriega's Panama, the part that the elections do not reach. In Yaviza, and a hundred places like it, politics is decided in the town's barracks, not in its polling station.

just like the night

THE EARLY summer of 1966: our last year at school. We lived for the music, lived in the beautiful landscape of 'pop'. We were playing *Aftermath* and *Otis Blue* and *Revolver*. We were ear-plugging through the static into Radio Lux. We were poring over *Rave* and *Record Mirror*.

Dylan was different, we knew that, but also he was part of this landscape. 'Exclusive colour pics' brought us the latest look: Cuban heels, black shades, high-tab collar, the wild halo of hair. It was the time of the great Dylan controversy: the folkies versus the rockers. In May he wound up his European tour at the Albert Hall. People heckled and booed when he played his electric set. Some of them walked out. I heard it

from *The Dylan Companion* (1990)

later on the bootleg: the folkies yell 'Judas' and Dylan says 'I don't *beleeve* you', and then this great rip-tide of music comes sweeping in behind him as the band moves into the intro of 'Like a Rolling Stone'.

At the time this controversy didn't mean much to us. This was 1966. Of *course* Dylan was playing electric.

We expected Dylan to surprise us, but *Blonde on Blonde* bewildered us. It almost scared us. We had heard the beauty and anger of his previous albums: now he hardly had time for either. *Blonde on Blonde* came from somewhere else, somewhere we didn't really want to be. Musically it couldn't be labelled: not folk, not pop, not country. The up-tempo songs like 'Leopard-skin Pill-box Hat' and 'Obviously Five Believers' were rough and spiky, but it wasn't the roughness we loved in the Stones and the Pretty Things. The slow songs carried you off like soul music.

The sweep and size of the album took our breath away. Four sides, fourteen songs, one lasting *a whole side*, a song full of questions you had no answer to:

> And with the child of the hoodlum
> wrapped up in your arms,
> How could they ever have persuaded you?

We know more about it now—that the 'Sad-eyed Lady' of the song was his wife Sara; that he stayed up for days in the Chelsea Hotel writing it; that it was recorded in one take, down in Nashville in February 1966, with a bunch of musicians who had hardly even heard of him until that evening—but we still don't have the answers.

The songs took us off into weird subterranean stories: amphetamines and pearls, guilty undertakers and riverboat captains, Honky Tonk Ruthie dancing beneath a Panamanian moon. We were schoolboys. We had never tasted railroad gin, never been anywhere like that, but Dylan spoke to us from there. That was what was scary: if you kept changing and questioning and pushing on through, as Dylan did, these were the places you ended up.

Even more than *Highway 61*, I think of *Blonde on Blonde* as opening up for us a whole new imaginative world. These places he sang from were inside his head, somewhere else to be, separate realities. Later we took drugs, but perhaps it was Dylan's poetry that first kicked us out of ourselves. The poetry and the music, coming out of its special twilight: the voice, the band, the harmonica blowing it all away at the end.

The song I always come back to is 'Visions of Johanna'. It's an hour-of-the-wolf song. It comes up out of some back-room of the soul. Dylan's smoky voice wraps around those long, long lines: 'But Mona Lisa must have had the highway blues, you can tell by the way she smiles.' Behind him, there's his night-owl band: Al Kooper on keyboards, Robbie Robertson on guitar, and Kenny Buttrey's drums, soft and feathery and somehow furtive, pacing quietly like footsteps in the hall.

In my mind this song is the anthem of my first all-nighters at school: sometimes solitary, sometimes with a few good friends, down in the gun-rooms with the lights on low and a towel under the door: Terence, Eddy, Nick, and me, and our unspoken leader Charlie Pilkerton.

Pilk had already *been there*: his parents were divorced, he had written a novel, he had read *The Waste Land*, above all he had gone all the way with a girl called Rhona. Maybe we never quite believed him, but on the matter of the music there could be no doubt. Pilk had some kind of hotline: he heard a new sound almost before it happened. He slips a new single out of its coloured envelope, feeds it on to the trusty Dynatron, flicks back his greasy fringe. 'This one's called "Hey Joe". This guy plays guitar with his *teeth . . .*'

It was Pilk who first had a copy of *Blonde on Blonde*, Pilk who plumbed its mysteries for us, Pilk who declared, puffing on a Perfectos at three in the morning, that 'I Want You' wasn't about a woman at all, it was about heroin.

In the night you were free. It was like hearing the sound of a train in the darkness, and suddenly you weren't under the bedclothes any more, you were on the train, gunning down the track through all those extra, secret hours. And then the dawn: putting out the lights, turning back to the communal day, heading off down the school's underground corridors known as Plug Street, carrying the untouchable secrets of your existence in a song.

Blonde on Blonde still holds its charge. It's still there to accompany you through whatever it might be that keeps you up past the dawn. Now that the controversies are over, now that you're older, you perhaps care less about the gesture of it, or the surreal extremities of the poetry. You see it now as a more human thing: a collection of love-songs, texts of betrayal and despair and supreme gallows-humour.

You also see it now as just a chapter of Dylan's story. Ahead lay the burn-out: even in our innocence we knew that burning out was what *Blonde on Blonde* was all about. Ahead lay the motorcycle crash, the 'Basement Tapes', *John Wesley Harding*. And then the Isle of Wight concert. That was the first time I saw Dylan. He wore a white suit and a scrubby beard. His hair was short, his voice was in its country comic-opera guise: 'Lay, Lady, Lay' time.

It was 1969. We were massed in this field, thousands of people, a shanty-town of polythene and blankets. We were there for him, but he was hardly there at all.

D**ESPITE THE** threat of rain, the hostility of the Mendip District Council, and the memories of ugly confrontations last summer, the Glastonbury CND Festival went ahead as planned, and some 80,000 people turned up to mark the summer solstice with a long weekend of revelry, music and epic squalor.

It was the seventh Glastonbury Festival since 1970, and the biggest yet. Proceeds to CND will easily top last year's festival earnings of £100,000. Some of the old-timers who remembered the first festival—an acid pastorale with a couple of thousand people there and the late Marc Bolan topping the bill—were saying that it had grown too big, lost its special qualities,

The Listener, 1987

become an all-purpose rock-and-roll beanfeast. Perhaps it is innocence that it's lost, and perhaps it had to. My worst fear, not having been to one of these festivals for years, was that it would all have ossified. A bunch of balding, yuppified rock-children trying to get a whiff of their glory days, and a tribe of superannuated pixies still prognosticating about the Age of Aquarius: that was my worst fear.

It wasn't like that at all. The crowd was eclectic in age, style and regional accent. People had come from all over the country: cashed their Giros and hitched down, left their worries and driven down, got moved on by the police and convoyed down. What hasn't been lost—or perhaps in these hard political times is being regained—is the strange coherence of these gatherings. The gathering itself becomes the event, a giant communal *coup de théâtre* in which everyone is a performer. People come for various reasons, but when the festival takes over, the only real reason for being there is simply to be there.

Though no doubt alarming for residents in the immediate vicinity, the festival's ability to invade and transform its venue is remarkable. For most of the year this is 20 acres of quiet Somerset farmland, a green combe looking west to Glastonbury Tor. Its pastures bear gnarled old names like Michael's Mead, Bottom Webb's Ash and Creep Ground. Then comes this week of madness. The hard core of the festival arrives mid-week: technicians and stall-holders, bikers and hippies, the 'New Age Gypsies' of the convoys. They colonise the lower slopes of the valley, overlooking the central stage, an 80-foot-tall pyramid emblazoned with the CND logo. (The pyramid's metal cladding, ironically, was Ministry of Defence surplus.) The weekenders filter in Friday evening, and by dusk on Saturday, the eve of the solstice, the transformation is complete.

LOOKING DOWN through the valley there is something mythic about the size and the ragged organic logic of the scene below. A small city has sprouted and sprawled up both sides of the valley, a smoky encampment of tents, benders, shacks and bike-circles. It looks like something distant in time and place— a medieval siege-camp, perhaps; or a Hindu festival; or a South American shanty-town in the throes of some terminal fiesta. The mud, the bonfires, the torchlight, the cacophony, the fry-stalls, the hawkers, the dogs, the wild-eyed children, the dreadful slamming of the cubicle doors around the midden-pits, the thousands of blanket-clad people grimed with dirt and radiant with exhaustion: what it decidedly *doesn't* look like is England in the late 1980s.

It isn't just a music festival. There is theatre and spectacle, a scrap-metal sculpture park, a children's area, and the celebrated Green Field. The latter is up on the south slope, an area set aside for peace and quiet and the re-creating of frazzled tissue. Here I had a homoeopathic head-massage from Rose, a soothing lady in a floral dress. Various diminutive stalls offered promises connected with polarity-healing, acu-pressure and auro-soma. There was a workshop session on 'rebirthing', but I felt that might be biting off more than I could chew.

Music is still the glue that binds the experience together.

The Festival has five music stages, on the go from noon to night. With so much to choose from you make a few firm dates, and leave the rest to random encounters with popular music of every hue and shade and from every continent. I was glad not to miss Billy Bragg, singing his latter-day-Digger songs in a packed, hushed tent in the early hours of Sunday morning. The African township-jive bands—Bhundu Boys and Jonah Moyo—were exhilarating. I enjoyed a masterfully tacky combo called the Screaming Abdabs.

In terms of billing, the musical climax was Van Morrison's performance: an enduring figure in the quick-fading annals of rock, a singer of huge power and richness. The sun went down behind the Tor on Sunday evening, the band struck up with a long jazzy intro to 'Moondance', and Van the Man moved huffily onto the stage, dressed for the evening like an ageing biker in black leather and tight jeans. To begin with we feared that he wasn't going to settle, but then he started to slap his guitar about, and let his voice roll and flow, and for a while he charmed us with the old gruff magic.

AND SO the festival ploughed on through the weekend. The drug-hawkers called their wares—microdots and mushrooms, black rocky and hot knives. The Rasta-man called his patter: 'Cider or beer or snake-bite style . . . Glaston-berry Medicay-shun . . . No mental problems involved.' The heroic crew of the Workers' Beer Co-operative gunned their tractor up the miry ways to deliver kegs of local ale to far-flung outposts. The sellers of sandwiches and veggieburgers, hash fudge and 'straight fudge' competed for attention.

On Monday morning the rain came back, the party was over, the circus pulled out. Everyone was exhausted and filthy but these seemed like tokens of the *realness* of the weekend. It wasn't freeze-dried or shrink-wrapped, it wasn't sheathed in a condom, it wasn't on the video, it hadn't been done up in bright snappy pastels and renamed Glasters. It was real and we had been there. We drove off home to our lives, the car too full for any of the line of bedraggled kids hoping for a lift. They held up signs with their destinations written on. One of them had a sign which said 'ANYWHERE'.

the big fight

I**T WAS** the night before Beauregard's big fight, time for his final preparations. Jo said I could come and watch but— he laid a black, sea-scoured finger to his lips—'no fool questions.' We left the lights of Vauclin and walked inland. The music from the Saturday night *baldoudou* faded. Jo began to sing. He would croon a few lines in his impenetrable Creole, and then it would be the turn of Georges and me to come in with the refrain:

> *Beauregard, Beauregard, Beauregay,*
> *Li bougé comme cou z'éclay . . .*

Granta, 1988

Beauregard himself was silent. He sat in state in a small cane-stem cage covered with a red cloth. Jo carried the cage with great care, despite all the rum he'd drunk.

Beauregard was a five-year-old fighting cock. This is a good age for a fighter: age was now part of his prowess. He was a *zinga*—a speckled grey—of Venezuelan extraction. Here in Martinique the cocks of Latin America are highly prized. They are nimble and cunning, *très méchant*. They are real *coq gime*—the Creolization of 'game cock'—as opposed to the barnyard mongrels that form the staple of West Indian cocking. Beauregard weighed in at about three pounds and, according to the song we sang, moved like a flash of lightning. He was the pride of Georges, his owner, and of Jo, who was the skipper of Georges's two boats and Beauregard's handler and trainer.

The season had recently begun. It runs from December to May, roughly the length of the dry season. Beauregard had cruised a couple of outings against local opposition, but to-morrow was the big one. This time it wasn't just Georges's money and Jo's esteem that were riding on him, but the prestige of the entire village. Tomorrow, at the cockpit on the edge of Vauclin, Beauregard would meet Tonton, the pride of Trois Ilets across the other side of the island. Rivalry was intense, and the pre-fight betting—not so much on the outcome, for everyone in Vauclin believed that Beauregard would take it, but on such niceties as the duration of the bout and the mode of the *coup de grâce*—had been going on all week.

So too had Beauregard's training. Three times a day he was brought to a shady corner of the yard to spar with another of

Georges's roosters. For sparring he wore a protective hood and leggings, made of sized sackcloth. Placing the hood on him, Jo called him *ti-moine*, little monk. After the spar Beauregard was put in a box in the corner of his pen and covered with straw to sweat. His pen was roomy and shaded by spreading catalpa trees. None of the other roosters lived in such style. He had four separate perches in the pen—a little bit of variety to lessen his *ennui*, for now that he was in training he was brought no hens to tread and was kept away from the daily business of the farmyard. The perches were carefully measured, each the length of the handle of Jo's machete. This encouraged the cock to perch with his feet close together. The cock that is *étroit* (narrow) strikes deadliest.

In a corner of the pen was a square of sand. Here Beauregard fed, so as not to blunt his beak on the packed earth of the yard. His day-to-day diet was cornseed and manioc meal, baked into small loaves. To this, various sharpeners were added, more and more as the fight neared. Eggs were beaten in, butter and molasses, zests of rum. He had hog-plum juice and bitter aloes to purge him, oleander leaf to harden his skin and a herb called *zo-poisson* (fish bone) for general good luck. And he had urine, poured from a little bottle into the mash. *Pipi ti-fi,* Jo was careful to specify. Little girl's pee.

That afternoon, a close clipping from Jo. His neck-hackle was cut back, leaving just a stumpy tonsure of black feathers around the crown, and a furrow of exposed pink skin down the neck and along the back. The purpose of this is to deny the opponent beak-hold: on some islands in the West Indies clipping the neck-hackle is disallowed. He also had his wings clipped a couple of inches, so he didn't fly up too high when striking. The spines of the wing-feathers were then sharpened with a knife, adding another weapon.

And now, the night before the fight, with the moon high and nearing the full, came the final preparation: we were taking him to Auguste.

WE LEFT the road. We walked along tracks, past banana groves and plots of cane and isolated farmhouses where dogs set up a racket. We were in a valley called the Coulée d'Or. The plumed tassels of the sugarcane waved gently, though I could feel no breeze. The air seemed still and heavy now we had left the sea.

Jo said the sugar harvest would soon begin. He had worked as a cutter on the neighbouring island of St Lucia, which was why he spoke some English, which was why he had befriended me, which was why I was here right now. We had a casual deal. Jo promised to 'show me life' in Vauclin; I paid for things along the way. Often this meant standing him rounds of rum at one of the waterfront bars, till his lean black face shone, and his peeling old topi slid down over his forehead, and he told me of the wife he had left in San Fernando, Trinidad, and of his daughter called Fête because she was born on Quatorze Juillet, and of the two children he had 'put in the ground', and then the talk would turn to Deborah, an American girl who had passed this way, and Jo would tell me once again that he had 'fucked Deborah no problem,' and at last it would be time to head unsteadily back, me to my room at the town's only hotel, the Auberge les Alizes, Jo to his wood and tin hut in the shanty streets of Pointe Athanase on the edge of Vauclin.

Jo took me out fishing for snapper and kingfish in *Tranquillité,* a twenty-foot dug-out with an outboard on the back. He cooked me sea-urchin stew. And he taught me the rudiments of Martiniquais Creole, a patchwork chassis of French, Spanish, English and Carib, powered along at breakneck speed by a stripped-down version of French syntax. One of the first Creolisms I learned was *bai-moin un ti-bagay,* 'give me a little something.' Tonight at the *baldoudou* Jo had been through many little somethings, on account of liquor and stakes at the dice stalls. The invitation to accompany him to Auguste's was something in return.

Auguste was what they call a *doctor feuille,* a 'leaf doctor'. The leaf doctor is a healer and minor shaman, a looker into the secrets of herbs and roots, a brewer of *quimbois* or magic potions. Auguste was one of several around Vauclin. When Jo first spoke of him earlier that evening he called him a *tonton macoute.* I was alarmed, thinking of Papa Doc's secret police in Haiti, but it turned out that the term, which literally means 'uncle satchel', originally referred to itinerant herbalists like Auguste.

We were taking Beauregard to Auguste to be blessed and coated with magic *quimbois.* Jo said this would assure his invincibility in the pit tomorrow against Tonton of Trois Ilets. Georges was less convinced. He was of a different generation and class from Jo. At 25 he was half Jo's age. His father was, according to Jo, the richest man in Vauclin. There was Indian blood in the family, trading blood. Georges owned farmland, a brick-built house, two boats and a beach buggy. He was educated. He spoke good French. He talked of under-development and the third world and post-colonialism. He laughed at these old superstitions and *quimboiseries*. 'It is the religion of slaves,' he said. But he came along just the same, out of politeness to Auguste, and to keep a close eye on his rooster's welfare.

Jo believed in it all. We were simply doing things 'according to the laws.'

The path began to climb through woodland. The volcanic Mount Vauclin loomed above us in the moonlight. Auguste lived in the foothills, where the flora were more various than down near the sea. After an hour we arrived. A clearing gave onto a farmyard: low buildings, acacia-wood fencing, dogs, pigs, chickens. A group of men played dominoes beneath a hurricane lamp. We heard the slap of the dominoes and the calling of the numbers as we came round the last bend.

There were brief greetings, but we kept on walking, round the back of the buildings to a lean-to shed built of wood and palm-thatch. There was candlelight inside, and voices. A little girl in a dirty white dress came running out, and behind her in the half-lit doorway stood a small, elderly man. He wore a short-sleeved white shirt and a pair of beach shorts. This was the leaf doctor.

I hadn't known what to expect. I knew he wasn't going to

be a full-blown Voodoo *houngan* of any sort. The ritual and lore of Martinique is basically Voodoo, but not like that of Haiti. Georges had been very clear: there would be no frothing ecstasies, no animal sacrifice, no walking on gilded splinters. I was disappointed all the same. Auguste looked like any old fisherman-farmer. He was a thin, knotty man with big hands that made cuffing movements as he spoke. His face was wrinkled, with a white stubble. His teeth were few and seemed to have grown bigger, like trees in a clearing. He was a little drunk, and since Georges was even now presenting him with a bottle of Mammy rum, he was likely to become more so.

We were introduced to a man and woman, Auguste's assistants, and went inside. The shack was bare. There were a couple of broken chairs and some boxes to sit on, a table with three candles on it, and a rough stone fireplace. A low shelf in the corner was covered with a cloth of the same vivid red as that on Beauregard's cage. Bunches of dried leaves and roots hung from the rafters. On the wall there was a calendar advertising a French shipping line. It was turned to the current month—wintry vistas of the Auvergne—but was several years out of date.

The main impact of the room was not seen but smelt: candlewax and dust, spices and herbs, aromatic smoulderings from the fire, and other things impossible to guess at.

Auguste had greeted me with a cordial grunt. But I soon gathered he objected to my presence. His Creole was even faster than Jo's, but I caught the word *blanc* a couple of times, and *métro,* which is what they call a Frenchman. Jo told him I was English, and a writer, and anyway I would have to stay because I couldn't find my way back alone. Georges produced more offerings from his bag: a pack of untipped Gauloises, a pair of custard-apples from his own orchard, and a wad of old-fashioned ten-franc bills.

Auguste swiftly lost interest in the troublesome *blanc*. He began to count the money, now and then licking his thumb with a large pink tongue. The money was not enough. There was an argument, Auguste itemizing expenses on his thick fingers, Georges shrugging and muttering, *'Eh, beh, Bon Dieu!'* It all seemed something of a formality, and soon enough Georges pulled out a few more francs from his back pocket.

Everything was in order. Auguste said, *'Bai-moin ti-poule.'* Jo took the cloth off the cage, undid the wicker latch, and reached the rooster out into the leaf doctor's drowsy shack.

AUGUSTE HELD Beauregard gently in both hands. He looked him over, viewed him at angles, as if he were thinking of making a purchase.

'He has a good small head,' he observed.

'Yes, he has the gypsy face,' Jo replied.

'His eye is fierce.'

'Yes, eye of fire.'

The rhapsody continued. His thigh was fat, his legs were hard, his claws were sharp, his cock-a-doodle-doo was *comme il faut* (a cock that crows too loud or too often is thought to be showy, not a true fighter).

I had heard the legends of his prowess, both pugnacious and amatory, but I had never been much impressed by Beauregard's appearance. He was a small, scraggy specimen compared to the barnyarders of England. His head was peppered with scars and puncture marks, souvenirs of the pit. The newest scabs were speckled white with alum used to cauterize the wounds. His docked wattles and misshapen feathers gave him a shifty, down-at-heel air. He looked like the avian equivalent of someone who would gladly cheat you of your last *sou*. But to the expert eye he was clearly a thing of grace, the stuff of cockpit legend.

Auguste turned him round and peered at his rump. Where the lower tail feathers had been clipped, the flesh showed through a livid red. Auguste seemed pleased.

'*Eh beh, eh beh, fout'i bel cul rouge!*' he said. What a lovely red arse he's got.

Auguste walked to the centre of the hut. He held the rooster with outstretched arms. He pointed him to each of the four corners of the hut. Then he turned him round and stared into his red eye and began to mumble something in a fast, high voice. Most of this was unintelligible to me. I heard the names of Beauregard and Tonton, and the word *gageure*, which means a bet and is here used for a cockfight. I heard snatches of dog Latin and a formulary phrase repeated many times: *Ouvri barne pour li-passé.* Open the gates and let him pass.

I whispered to Georges, 'What's he saying?'

'He is praying to Gaspard.'

'Who is Gaspard?' An angry look from Jo. I had promised 'no fool questions'.

Georges smiled. Gaspard was a spirit, he whispered, a *capitaine des zombis* who had special influence in cock fights.

Auguste now went to the table. He asked for matches and lit the three candles on the table. There was old wax beneath them. He mumbled another imprecation in his high, irritable voice. The candles, I later learned from Georges, were lit in honour of another captain of the zombies, Agrippa.

Next came the preparing and applying of the magic *quimbois*. The red cloth was removed from the shelf in the corner, revealing many small piles: leaves, seeds, roots, pastes, parings and unguents. I recognized ginger and pimiento, and pods of vanilla, and the cuttings of purple verbena whose vivid blackcurrant aroma I had already smelt in the hut, but the rest were unknown to me. In the lore of *quimboiserie* I was illiterate. To one side lay a clutter of aged kitchenware—tin dishes, plastic funnels, bottles, dibbers. There was an ox tongue, looking none too fresh, in one of the dishes. Another contained chicken giblets.

Auguste began to mix and grind the ingredients in a small plastic bowl. He instructed his assistants, speaking in a calm, precise voice, like a surgeon. Dicings of tongue, a chicken's heart, a couple of pinches of scarlet snuff. Out of a small stoppered phial came a fine grey-black powder. I thought I caught a whiff of cordite. A dash of indigo, some cinammon bark, a pale yellow liquid that may have been more of the little girl's pee. He spat into the mix from time to time and dropped ash from his cigarette. The end product was a liverish blue-brown sludge. Some white spirit was added to make it easier to apply.

Beauregard was brought once more from his cage. Auguste scooped *quimbois* from the bowl and smeared it over him, working it in between his feathers. Beauregard protested. The *quimbois* stung his newly plucked skin, and though Jo held him tightly he twice managed to peck Auguste's hand. The leaf doctor just laughed, showing yellow teeth like tombstones.

We left around midnight. Jo and Georges argued. It seemed there was another ceremony which Jo had wanted Auguste to do. Georges hadn't wanted it. It was a bad ceremony, he said, and anyway Auguste charged too much. It involved the use of *poussiére de mort,* 'dead man's dust', taken from a grave in the local cemetery.

The night had grown heavy and hot. Suddenly Jo stopped. 'Listen' he said. He cupped his hand to his ear and rolled his eyes. Above the night sounds I heard a strange, low, creaking kind of moan. It might have been the wind, but none was blowing. It might have been a woman groaning softly by the roadside.

Jo saw my startled face and doubled up in laughter. Georges said, 'It's OK, it's just the banana trees.' At certain times of the year they groan as the sap is forced down into the fruit. It was the groaning of the *bananiers,* nothing more.

SUNDAY AFTERNOON and the cockpit was filling up fast. A fat mama in polka dots took the money at the door: ten francs for the front row, eight for the rest. She moved with surprising agility to collar two boys trying to worm up through the benches without paying.

The cockpit, Le Pitt Atlantique, was a circular wooden structure covered with a tin roof. From the outside it resembled one of those early playhouses you see in maps of Elizabethan London. There were no walls, just tiered wooden benches around the arena, which was a circle of packed earth about thirty feet in diameter. The pit stood on land owned by Georges's father. We had eaten lunch at his home: rum punch on the balcony, fresh snapper and plantain cakes. In his front room were reproduction Gauguins and a row of encyclopaedias locked in a glass-fronted bookcase. He had lost the key some years ago. 'I'm too old to learn anyway,' he said.

We went inside the cockpit. There was shade and the hum of voices. Smoke drifted in from the fry-stalls outside. Around the arena the faces were packed in tight. So many black faces under so many hats: trilbies and Panamas and *bakoua* straw hats; Jo's old topi and Georges's orange baseball cap with 'Honda' written on it; the women's headscarves of bright Madras cotton, knotted to signal a heart that is free (one knot), a heart that is taken (two knots), a heart that is anybody's (three knots). Some of the women were so lovely you hardly dared to count.

The luminaries of Vauclin life were there: Pierre the melancholy butcher; Ti-Noēl the boat-builder, another of Jo's candidates for the richest man in the village; Monsieur Fragonard the policeman, a small pallid Parisian said to be on the run from his past; and Christophe, the *patron* of the hotel, big and jovial and bearded like a pirate, cradling in his arms his pet mongoose, Papetu, whose trick was to bite my toes beneath the dining table until I delivered bits of bread and cheese.

The bookmakers were ranged along the front row, dapper in pressed shirts and sunglasses, with thin cigars between their teeth. Bets were shouted from all sides, computed in the old French style, *cent* for one franc and *mille* for ten. Hands waved fans of banknotes, hands did tic-tac, hands wiped the sweat from gamblers' brows.

The first bout was about to get underway. Two cocks were brought into the arena. They were 500-gram bantam cocks: the smallest birds go first. Their weights were confirmed, and chalked up on a blackboard. A wooden box, fastened to the roof by a rope and pulley, was let down into the arena. It contained a candle, a cake of wax, some cotton wool, a bottle of alcohol and sticking plaster. First each cock was swabbed with alcohol to clean any grease or remnants of *quimbois* from its feathers. Next some wax was heated with the candle and pressed onto the cock's heel. Spurs were fastened on with the wax and held in place by the plaster.

The spurs were steel, about two inches long, tapering to a vicious point. Jo had told me that in the old days they used to be silver, but now 'no one has the knowledge to make them.' The spur was fixed to the shaved-down stub of the cock's natural spur. The handler must be careful to get the angle exactly right. The action of a cock when 'heeling' an opponent brings the spurs close to his own head, and there is the risk of him gashing himself if they are wrongly mounted.

The preliminaries were complete. The referee was satisfied.

'Hors la gageure!' The handlers carried the cocks out of the ring. The box of accoutrements was winched back to the roof. Two little doors opened at opposite sides of the arena. The cocks were ushered through, the doors slammed shut behind them, and the fight was underway.

IT IS gone five when Beauregard and Tonton at last take the ring. The light softens outside the Pitt Atlantique, but inside the heat is raging. A succession of cocks—Montagne, Danse, Emmanuel, Passepartout, Ti–Diable ('Little Devil'), Longé Di-ole ('Stick out your beak') and many others—have come and gone and fought their brief encounters, one lasting no more than forty seconds before he was pierced through the lung and tossed to the mounting pile of corpses in the corner.

But no thought of these now as—weighed, swabbed, spurred and given a quick shot of *rhum vieux* through a straw—the two old campaigners enter the cockpit.

Tonton is brown with orange streaking on his saddle-feathers. His true name is Napoleon, fitting enough since Trois Ilets is the birthplace of Marie-Joseph Taschers, better known as Napoleon's Josephine. Tonton—'Uncle'—is a nickname of-ten given to veteran fighters. His handler is a big man. He has a flat, squarish face, the look of a hammerhead shark.

The opening of the fight follows an established pattern. First, the sizing-up. Beauregard is nonchalant. He saunters round his patch of the pit as if it were a corner of his own well-appointed pen. He pecks at a few imaginary morsels in the dust. He peers with mild curiosity at the antics of the crowd. He doesn't seem to have noticed Tonton at all. Tonton's style is different. He is brisk, muscular, confident. He patrols his patch, limbers, flexes his wings. I half expect him to do a few quick press-ups.

By degrees the combatants draw closer to each other. Tonton moves in a busy zigzagging path. He's got energy to spare. Beauregard is still casual, musing, his little tonsured head moving back and forth like a well-oiled mechanism. As they meet the noise mounts. A contingent of visitors from Trois Ilets is packed in close to the entrance, battling to be heard above the home crowd. *'Va, Va, salope!'* shout the Vaucliniers. *'Bai-li, bai-li, bai-li!'* bellow the Insulaires.

The opening flurries are exploratory. They are warning shots: a quick angry mingling, a dance of feathers. The crowd affects to find this hilarious. There are shouts of *'Yo baissé comme ti-fi!'* ('They're kissing like little girls') and *'Yo chanté pomme, Bon Dieu!'* ('They're sweet-talking each other').

The cocks separate. In more natural circumstances this first scuffle might have settled the argument. But there is no room for diplomacy in the *gageure*. Beauregard seems to turn away, as if to return to his corner. Then suddenly he is springing, up and at Tonton. Tonton rises too, but a second late. There's a vicious session of hacking and pecking. For a moment they hang there, a blur of wings and dust high above the ground. They push away and fall. Beauregard lands with absurd aplomb, while Tonton lurches down in a lopsided movement. First blood to Beauregard.

Down in the handlers' area Jo is haggard-faced. He shouts,

waves his topi, runs a hand through his cropped grey hair. Georges is silent, leaning his elbows on the wooden rim of the arena, chewing fast on some gum. Across the other side Hammerhead from Trois Ilets looks worried. He waves a huge fist at the cocks, issues dark ultimata.

Beauregard has the best of the second skirmish but Tonton takes the third. He produces an extraordinary swivelling movement in mid-air and delivers a deadly reverse-heel kick. His spurs rake down Beauregard's neck. Of the cock's two weapons, beak and spurs, it is the spurs which are the killers. The beak can blind, and it can finish off a downed cock, but its main use in the *gageure* is to get hold of the opponent's head so that the spurs can do their business. Beauregard reels away. There is blood and torn skin on his back. For a moment it seems that Tonton might turn the tables.

It is not to be. Tonton is tough and cunning, but after half a dozen skirmishes there is little doubt. Both birds are dazed now, but it is Beauregard who is relentless, wheeling into the next attack while Tonton is still recovering from the last.

This is the finale. Tonton is exhausted. His movements are weary. He has forgotten why he is here. A few last jabs with the spur and he is down. Beauregard turns on his heel, struts to the crowd, punch-drunk. His beak is full of blood and feathers, and the feathers flutter out as he crows a few cracked war-cries. The red light flashes on and off ten times and Tonton is counted out.

The fight has lasted four minutes. People call, *'Net, net, net!'*—the equivalent of the football crowd's chant of 'Ea-sy!'—

as the handlers run on to gather up the roosters. Tonton is still moving: perhaps he'll pull through. The bookies are beginning to pay out. Jo examines Beauregard, looking for the bad wounds. Then he puts the rooster's head in his mouth and sucks it to clean off the blood, and for a moment there's a silence in my head, and when the noise comes flooding back I find myself shaken.

I did not think I was that kind of person: another voice yelling for blood, another face craning to see the kill.

I walk down to the handlers' area. They're mobbing Jo, thrusting drinks at him, brandishing their winnings. Everyone looks happy. Beauregard quivers in his cage. The blood on his torn back is the colour of the cloth on his cage, the colour of the cloth on the leaf doctor's shelf.

crows

THE SNOW came late and deep to the Corvedale. The operations of spring were suspended. For our children it was a paradise, but for the sheep-farmers it was a disaster. They were out all day and half the night, struggling up to their stranded flocks, carrying up feed and carrying down dead lambs.

We climbed Bouldon Ridge and looked down over the valley. Patches of colour broke through the snow: the sepia line of hedgerows, the apricot flare of budding poplars. In the distance we could see the rookery next to our house. It was late afternoon, the hour of commotion. We watched the birds rising and wheeling and settling back down, like specks of black paper over a bonfire.

1990

We were too far away to hear them, but I could hear other rooks nearby. They were above us, just the other side of the hazel coppice that ran below the ridge-top. They were making a racket of alarm: I thought we must have disturbed them, our voices carrying across the stillness.

We came up through the tweedy brown coppice, and out into high pasture. And then we saw them: twenty birds, perhaps more—it was impossible to count them—caught in a crow-trap.

The trap was simple: a large rectangular hutch built of wood and wire-netting. The entrance was in the roof, an angled funnel of netting. It was just big enough for a bird to get down it, but the angle made any return impossible. They were mostly rooks, but there were a few carrions in there with them. It was a strange, mediaeval vision: a cage of black birds in an empty white field. They were frantic with hunger. The temperature was already near freezing. The bait, whatever it was, had long since been eaten up.

I had a knife. I could have cut the netting and freed them. It was a debatable point whether I ought to. Crows are an enemy: they are not my enemy, but in these conditions they are certainly the sheep-farmer's enemy. They compete for the feed, they prey on weakened animals, and sometimes—so one was told—they take the eyes out of lambs which are still being born. These were the grim fortunes of war we were seeing here.

I do not know if this alone would have stopped me. What stopped me was fear. I was quite certain that if we opened up the trap, the crows would come swarming out and attack us. They would try and kill us. They would take out the eyes of my children. I was probably wrong, but there was an intensity of anger inside that trap, a dark rage, which scared the hell out of me.

The trap was another small chapter in an old, old story of persecution. Everything about the crow is old. They look like they have been here forever, an archetypal presence in the landscape. Our words for them—crow, rook, daw, chough— are imitative. They are early, rudimentary words: echoes as much as names.

Their features are unlovely, their habits unpleasant, their song 'poor and raucous'. Everything goes into the business of survival. There are few corners of the world where this bullying omnivore has not found a niche. There are rookeries in the steppes of Central Asia, and white-necked ravens scavenging the African bush. I have seen the handsome, speckled nut-cracker in the pine-woods of Dalmatia, and the large-billed crow fishing like an ungainly black gull off the coast of the Malay peninsular.

In Scotland the hooded crow predominates, with its pale silver-grey tunic. On Skye once we saw one circling over a patch of cliffside scrub. 'There'll be another one down below,' said the boatman. They hunt in pairs, he explained: one of them stays up to keep a look-out. 'He's a canny old bird, the hoodie.'

When I was a child I much admired the ravens at the Tower of London, and loved the sonorous name of their keeper, the

Yeoman Ravenmaster. There is a complement of six birds, but by tradition there are also two 'guest ravens'. When a raven dies, it is buried in the moat near Traitor's Gate. A famous Tower bird, James Crow, was in residence for forty four years.

The birds amuse themselves by chipping out mortar from the Tower walls and dropping it on the cars parked below. Similar destructive habits were noted by Charles Dickens, who kept a pet raven. The bird lived in the stable, and mimicked the language of grooms and coachmen. 'He would perch outside my window,' Dickens recalled, 'and drive imaginary horses, with great skill, all day.' He was the model for Grip, the raven in *Barnaby Rudge*.

Standing there on Bouldon Ridge I remembered watching the ravens being shut up for the night in their cage near the Wakefield Tower. It was a very well-appointed cage: each bird had his own compartment, with louvred doors and straw bedding. Across the years the two images met: a frisson of fear that seemed to pass, like a crackle of electricity, from my childhood to this moment with my own children beside me.

We watched the crows for a while, but our curiosity seemed impertinent. The least we could do was leave them in peace. A few of the birds had settled down on the floor of the trap, exhausted and resigned. They would all die that night, taking their secrets with them.

biographical note

C HARLES NICHOLL was born in London in 1950 and studied at King's College, Cambridge. In the early 1970s he worked as a journalist for the London *Daily Telegraph* and the *Andean Times* of Lima, and was a British correspondent for *Rolling Stone*. His first book, *The Chemical Theatre,* was published in 1980. He is the author of several books of history, biography and travel, whose subjects range from Colombian drug-smugglers (*The Fruit Palace*) to Elizabethan pamphleteers (*a Cup of News*). His historical detective-work in *The Reckoning*, about the murder of the dramatist Christopher Marlowe, won him the James Tait Black Prize and the Crime Writers' Association 'Gold Dagger' award. His most recent book, *Somebody Else: Arthur Rimbaud in Africa,* was awarded the 1998 Hawthornden Prize. He lives in Italy with his wife and children.